To
Rose
Best
Wish

Steve

SHEA ARENDER
ILLUSIONS OF THE KING

A Magical Journey - Life as Elvis Presley

JEC PUBLISHING COMPANY

2969 E. Chestnut Expy.

Springfield, Missouri 65802

(800) 313-5121

www.jecpubco.com

First Edition

Library of Congress Control Number: 2010931780

ISBN: 978-0-9828531-1-5

Author: Shea Arender

Cover Design by: Gene Hamil

Edited by: Pam Eddings

Editing Contributions by: Ken Raggio

Prepared for Publishing by: JE Cornwell and Carolyn Cambronne

Printed in USA

Acknowledgements

Thank you Gene Shaw, Steve Wade, Wayne Carman (Elvis' Karate Legacy) and Legacy Entertainment Inc. Also thanks to Kyle Toney and production staff.

Thank you Gene Hamil of Event Screamer LLC for great concert photos and video production and a special thanks to World Health Industries.

Thanks CC Rider Band, Richard Smith, Rick Moreira, John Mason, Phil Sherrer and Jeff Pinter, for many great years of dedication on the road and in the recording studio.

Thank you to all my family, friends and fans for all the years of support. It's been an awesome journey. Without you all, my mission would be impossible.

Thank you JEC PUBCO Staff: Pam Eddings for your knowledge, hard work and dedication. A special thanks to JE Cornwell and Carolyn Cambronne for layout and Ken Raggio for editorial support.

God Bless,

Shea Arender

Table of Contents

Chapter 1

Connections To The King

A man only has one life to live. This one was born in the shadow of Elvis Presley. That was sometimes a dark curse; at other times, an angelic blessing. Shea Arender embraced his passion for life on his King's journey, and it took him to the furthest corners of the world with his "Tribute to the King," and "Illusional Journey."

"It is more than just a tribute. What I do represents my state, my people, and the birthplace of America's music," Arender says.

Arender's journey down "the King's" path began when he was just twelve years old. While he was aboard a Commodore Cruise in the Caribbean with his family, the passengers were offered the opportunity to play as extras and stage hands for "The History of Rock-'n-Roll" show, which was filmed during the voyage.

Young Shea immediately signed up. "I had to fill out an application form. For my 'experience,' I wrote down 'dancing, singing and Elvis,'" Arender said. "I was a just a kid, so when I showed up, the producers politely laughed at me. I could tell they didn't take me seriously. But they took my name and information, and fortunately, they called me a day later. Their Elvis guy was sick and could not return to the stage."

When Arender auditioned, he wore his "Jailhouse Rock" shirt. The dark-brown-haired youth spoke with a natural Southern drawl, and he danced and moved just like Elvis. He was immediately cast in the show, and the producers' introduction of him was: "Well folks, this is our Elvis!"

The show played to more than 1,000 passengers, and producers were worried that Arender might freeze up in front of the crowd. He admits he was terrified. His parents knew that, too. However, they knew something the producers didn't know; that Arender was well-prepared to play Elvis.

He had started working on his Elvis portrayal just for fun when he was only seven years old, after his mother bought him a tape of Elvis' Golden Records and Elvis' "Loving You" movie. Listening to Presley's music and watching the King's movies became a passion for the young man.

While reminiscing of those days, Arender said, "I was obsessed with Elvis. While other kids were playing video games, I studied Elvis' music and movies, singing his songs and learning his moves. I spent many hours a day for three or four years to get all those moves down. By the age of ten or eleven, I had perfected his moves; but I didn't get the voice down until I was almost eighteen."

During rehearsals aboard ship, the director told Arender how to move his body in "Jailhouse Rock," but Arender quickly and confidently let him know that the choreography was not correct. "I knew every move Elvis made in 'Jailhouse Rock.' I also knew the dancers' moves, their positions on stage, ...everything," he said. When he realized the choreographers and dancers didn't know the exact moves, Arender was compelled to show them how to do it right.

The show used a live band as well as music and vocals in the background – sort of a sing-a-long effect – so Arender didn't have to worry that he hadn't quite developed the Elvis voice he would later perfect. "I pulled it off. I knew then that I had it in me to perform Elvis' music," Arender said.

The entertainment travel company that booked the deal agreed, and years later told Arender that his show had remained one of the most requested videos in the company's history.

After the Commodore Cruise in 1992, Arender was hooked on show business. It was a natural progression for the young man to develop an Elvis act, because his family and friends always said that he looked like Elvis.

His first memories of music and early childhood stories were about Elvis. His sister-in-law's mother, Anita Wood Brewer, dated Elvis from 1957 until 1962. Arender had known Anita his whole life, so he had heard countless stories, and had seen much memorabilia and original photographs of Elvis around the house in those days.

Arender dedicated himself to working on his Elvis act. "I wasn't shy. I was a liberal arts dude with a football attitude." Growing up in a small town, Arender was somewhat of an oddity, which occasionally caused tough kids to make fun of his artistic ways. However, Arender quickly put a stop to that. "I could sing and take care of myself if I had to," he said. "I am a mix of just enough testosterone, and a hint of rugged Cajun redneck."

He took advantage of every opportunity to perform as Elvis. Throughout the South, he could be seen in county fairs, parties, community events, or anywhere else he received an invitation. When Arender started doing his act in the early 1990s, others were doing Elvis impersonations for recreation or for shows in Las Vegas. However, nobody took the role to the level that Arender did. Being an Elvis Tribute Artist is a true and serious profession for Arender; a role he strives to portray with honor, respect and absolute accuracy.

While working to perfect his act, Arender added to his knowledge about Presley by visiting Elvis' former girlfriend, Anita Wood Brewer, and by calling on Presley's friends and former staff members in Memphis.

"Anita opened the door for me to meet people like George Klein, for instance."

As a Humes High School classmate and friend of Presley's, Klein traveled with the King during the 1950s before leaving to become a popular disc jockey at Memphis radio station WHBQ.[1] Presley and Kline remained lifelong friends, and each served as best man at the other's wedding.

Anita Brewer, who grew up in Jackson, Tennessee, first met Elvis after Presley and Klein saw her on a television show. From the moment

Presley saw her on television, he wanted to meet the lovely young blonde. "She was beautiful. She was smokin' hot," Arender said.

As Arender continued to perform his Elvis tribute act, his connections to the King grew. "It was amazing. Elvis's former entourage, bodyguards, fans from high school and other entertainers would come to concerts, get back-stage passes, and identify themselves," Arender said. "They'd show up anywhere from Las Vegas to Miami, or sometimes they would show up in small-town theaters in rural cities, and also on my Elvis tribute cruise. It was absolutely incredible."

Cruisin' With the King

Arender's Elvis-themed cruise, "Cruisin' with the King," is an exclusive annual cruise featuring Arender as Elvis. He performs as Presley in all of the King's musical eras – from Elvis' 1950s Rockabilly era; the King's 1960s era, which includes Elvis' 1968 comeback tour; to the 1970s jumpsuit era Elvis. "This is very difficult to do vocally. It is more difficult to portray the young Elvis when you are much older than forty. For me, in fifteen years it will be more challenging to do the young Elvis."

---

1 "My Life With Elvis," by Becky Yancey with Cliff Linedecker, p11. St. Martin's Press, New York, NY, © 1977.

Presenting illusions of Elvis on the first cruise provided a welcome challenge for Arender, not only in showcasing his skills as a vocalist and entertainer, but also by allowing him to get to know his fans better. He also got to use his Portuguese and Spanish language skills by talking with fans from other countries. It was during the cruise that Arender first learned that his CD, "American Trilogy," was on sale via Amazon in Germany and Japan. "My CD had reached across international borders. Meeting fans from all over the world was exciting. Overall, it was a great experience," Arender said.

When film clips of Elvis were projected on a big screen at the beginning of the Cruisin' with the King show, the crowd of more than one thousand fans went wild. "I had chills running up and down my spine because the crowd was so excited. I rocked it when I hit the stage," Arender said. "It seemed the international fans were more excited about the show than the American ones."

Then when he told the crowd he was from the South – from the same area where Elvis was from – they really went crazy. "A lot of people don't really think of Elvis the way that people from other countries do because Elvis was from around here; he grew up in our back yards. But for somebody from Germany or Spain, it is a dream to come here and walk the same streets that Elvis walked; and to see an American Tribute Artist from the South perform as Elvis," Arender said.

The foreign fans have great curiosity about Arender. They are fascinated with the fact that he is so young, yet has such extensive knowledge of Elvis and his music. That opens the door for him to talk about his family history and personal connections to the King. Then they are eager to purchase his "American Trilogy" CD if they don't already own it.

American Trilogy

In 2007 Arender recorded the "American Trilogy" CD for Timeless Records at a small studio in Louisiana. Although modern technology was readily available for recording, mastering and engineering the CD, Arender didn't want to go that route with it. "I didn't want it to be recorded with all the bells and whistles – all the technology. I wanted it to be as authentic as possible; not so modern," Arender said.

The CD is a compilation of ten different songs – five recorded in the studio and five recorded live in concert. Although Arender has recorded more than fifty of the same songs Elvis recorded, he chose songs for his album that typified the range of the King's material. "I wanted a mix of Blues, Country, Rock, and some of Elvis' classic material," Arender said. The live recordings on the CD had minimal digital mastering. However, Arender's vocals have absolutely no digital enhancement or alterations, which is precisely the way he wanted the CD to be produced. "The sound is just the way I sound live," he says. "I wanted the CD to show my natural skills and abilities without dressing it up."

Arender was equally particular about the era and style of the songs included on "American Trilogy." For example, track five on the CD, 'Can't Help Falling in Love,' is the version of the song from Elvis' comeback special in 1968, rather than a version of the original, which was recorded by Presley in 1961.

Track six on the CD, 'Trouble,' was originally recorded by Elvis in 1958. For his CD, Arender did his own version and arrangement of 'Trouble.' "I took the 1958 and 1968 versions and combined them together," Arender said. He recorded 'Trouble' live in the studio, ad-libbing some of the arrangement.

Arender's version of 'Heartbreak Hotel,' track seven on "American Trilogy," was recorded live on Bourbon Street in New Orleans. The arrangement is jazz-influenced, featuring an additional guitar solo and two saxophone solos. "Because the original release of 'Heartbreak Hotel' in 1956 was only two minutes long, I chose a jazzy arrangement of the song as a tribute to the history of New Orleans," Arender said.

The last three cuts on "American Trilogy" were recorded live in Memphis during Elvis week, a celebration that annually brings more than 75,000 people to the city.

Other cuts on the CD include, 'You Gave Me a Mountain,' 'For the Good Times,' 'Kentucky Rain,' and 'Suspicious Minds.'

Something you won't hear on the CD is the well-known tagline from Elvis' performances: "Elvis has left the building."

"A lot of people ask why I do not say, 'Elvis has left the building' at the end of the recording," Arender said. "I didn't want to use it because Elvis is dead, and my CD is a tribute to Elvis through my eyes. I don't want the last thing heard on my CD is 'Elvis has left the building.'"

Songs among those recorded but not selected for "American Trilogy" include: 'It's Now or Never,' from the 1960s and 'Don't Cry Daddy' from the early 1970s. Arender recorded 'My Way' and 'Hurt' because he loves the way Elvis hits the high notes on those songs. "I love to hit those high notes," Arender says. "It's a treat for me because Elvis' voice is phenomenal on those songs."

Arender has also recorded 'Soldier Boy,' a song of special significance to Arender, and to Mrs. Anita Wood Brewer. "I recorded that song as a dedication to Anita because it is one of her favorites. She told me when Elvis first heard that song, he said it made him think about her, and even to this day, she always gets a warm feeling about Elvis when she hears it," Arender said. Presley recorded 'Soldier Boy' in 1960.

And so the story begins. Here is the rest of the story, in Shea's own words.

Chapter 2

Anita Marie Wood Brewer

Memories of Elvis as told to Shea Arender

Anita Wood Brewer is a longtime friend and member of my family, and she has played a key role in my connections to the 'King.' Throughout my life she has told stories and shared photographs, letters and mementos from Presley with me.

Anita said that the first time she saw Elvis Presley in person, he stole her breath away. "He was effervescent … absolutely the best-looking man I'd ever seen before or since." When Presley picked her up for their first date, he was wearing a red velvet shirt, black trousers and a black motorcycle cap.[1]

The first time Anita Wood Brewer saw me, Shea Arender, dressed to portray Elvis, she reacted as if she had been hit by a bolt of electricity. She said the way I talked and looked reminded her so much of Elvis that she found my resemblance to Elvis to be unsettling – almost disturbing.

To this day the memories of Presley I evoke for Anita – powerful memo-

1 "Baby, Let's Play House" by Alanna Nash. © 2010, Harper Collins Publishers, New York, NY. p.236

ries of Elvis' and Anita's faded love from nearly 50 years ago -- are almost more than the aged beauty can bear. I always try to tone down my mannerisms and resemblance to Elvis when I am around Anita, out of respect to her and her husband, former football great Johnny Brewer.

Anita and Elvis dated from 1957 to 1962. In fact, she was Elvis' first serious girlfriend. They were so serious about each other that they even came up with names for their future children together. If they had a girl, they would name her Lisa Marie, and if they had a boy, they would name him Elvis Jr.

Marie is Anita's middle name, and it is also a family name. Several women in the family are named Marie, or have the middle name of Marie.

When I was about six or seven years old, my mother, LaShara Arender, often took me with her to visit Anita. When Anita saw me, she would say, "There is my Li'l Elvis!" During visits, my mother would read love letters aloud that Elvis and Anita had written to each other when they were apart. The thing I most remember about those letters was that Elvis used baby talk words in his writing to her.

 Baby talk was the special language Elvis and his mother, Gladys, used to talk to each other. Elvis called Anita 'baby' and talked to her in baby talk, just like he did to his mother. "I just ate that up, Anita said. "You know, who wouldn't?"

I loved those visits with Anita. Not only was I star-struck by Anita's beauty and mesmerized by her stories about Presley, but I was also fascinated because Anita had been a bona-fide movie star – she was an accomplished singer and dancer, and she had recorded songs at Sun Records in Memphis.

Meeting Elvis And His Family

Elvis first saw Anita on a local Memphis television show, "Top Ten Dance Party," which was hosted by Wink Martindale. Presley and a group of friends would usually watch the Saturday afternoon show in Graceland's basement television room. George Klein, a Memphis disc jockey and good friend of Presley's since eighth grade, was a friend of Martindale, who was also a Memphis disc jockey.

Aside from the music on "Dance Party," which was an American-Bandstand type of show, one of the attractions was the good-looking female co-host that Martindale had working with him. Klein had been telling Presley about the latest co-host, a pretty, young girl named Anita Wood from Jackson, Tennessee. Klein had met Wood through Martindale, and Martindale knew Wood because they were both from Jackson, Tennessee. In addition to her blonde hair and great figure, she had intelligence, a fine sense of humor, and a warm bubbly personality.[2]

After watching the show one Saturday afternoon, Presley asked Klein to call Anita and ask her for a date.

When Klein called, Anita turned him down – she already had a date for that evening. After Anita had to decline a second date, she figured she would never get another chance to go out with Presley; however, Klein called again, and Anita didn't have plans. She said "yes."

Several of Presley's friends – Klein, Lamar Fike and Cliff Gleaves (a Jackson, Tennessee resident and acquaintance of Anita) - went with Presley on the couple's first date. Presley drove his big black Cadillac limousine over to pick her up at the boardinghouse where she lived. Anita rented a room from a Memphis lady named Mrs. J.R. Patty. When Klein went to the door to pick up Anita for the date, Mrs. Patty, a proper Southern lady, refused to allow Anita to go with Presley until the young man came to the door himself. Mrs. Patty told Klein that if "Elvis were a real gentleman, he'd come up here and pick her up himself."

When Klein went back to the car and told Presley what Mrs. Patty said, Presley laughed, hopped out of the car and went up to the door.

2 "Elvis: My Best Man" by George Klein. © 2010 Crown Publishing Group, a division of Random House, New York, NY. p. 85

Their first date consisted of driving to pick up a sack of hamburgers from Chenault's Drive-In, driving around Memphis for a bit – including driving past the theater where Presley's movie, "Loving You," would be opening the next night –then concluding the evening with a visit to Graceland.

"He gave me a tour of Graceland and introduced me to his parents and his grandmother," Anita said. "We visited, listened to music, played the piano and sang together for awhile. Before I left, he gave me a pink and black Teddy bear."

Anita and Elvis began to date steadily after that. Klein described their relationship as "the steadiest and most serious relationship Elvis had had up to that point."[3] Anita said that Presley nicknamed her "Little," or "L'il Bit," because of her small size.

Anita described her dates with Elvis as lots of fun, with lots of laughter and practical jokes. They did simple things, like driving around, going out for burgers at Chenault's, where a special dining room was reserved for them in the back; watching movies at Graceland and at the Memphian Theater; going to the Fairgrounds to ride the Dodgem cars and the Pippen roller coaster; playing badminton, riding horses, going to McKellar Lake; roller skating at the Rainbow Rollerdrome; and making plans for their future together.

Elvis and Anita weren't the only ones making plans for their future. Presley's mother, Gladys, also wanted to see the couple marry.

Anita reminisced, "Gladys would talk to me about us getting married. She would say, 'You're just the girl for him. I know that you would take care of him, and he would always remember his roots and where he came from.' She would dream about us having a little boy and naming him Elvis Jr. She would say, 'I can just see him running up and down the driveway in his little bare feet, this little blonde-headed boy.' We talked about things like that a lot."

3 "Elvis: My Best Man" by George Klein. © 2010 Crown Publishing Group, a division of Random House, New York, NY. p. 86

When Presley left on August 27, 1957, for a whirlwind tour of the Pacific Northwest preceding his September 5-7 recording session, Anita was the center of attention at the train station. "Anita is number one with me – strictly tops," Presley said to the press and crowd that came to see him off. Elvis kissed Anita twice for the photographers and about five times for himself before he boarded the train.[4]

Anita had just won the Mid-South Hollywood Star Hunt, and she was traveling to New Orleans by train for the finalists' competition. The winner of the competition was promised a small movie role.

Presley's sold-out tour was wildly successful – perhaps too much so; the show in Vancouver ended in a riot, in which crazed fans tipped over the stage. Presley went on to the recording session after the tour. In the interim, Anita called Elvis to announce that she had won the competition and was on her way to Hollywood. The couple planned to meet in California the following week.

Gifts From The King

After Anita arrived in Hollywood, Elvis showed her around the city, and then presented her with a "friendship" ring, which has been described as a very expensive ring - 18 sapphires surrounding a large diamond. Presley purchased the ring at the Beverly Wilshire Jewelry Shop.[5]
In addition to the ring, which Anita's only daughter now owns and always wears, Elvis gave Anita other gifts. "He was very generous," she said. "He always offered to buy things for me and others, but I tried not to take advantage of his generosity."

Presley bought Anita a 1956 Ford, several pieces of jewelry, a poodle, and one year for Christmas he even bought her a guitar which had an inlaid gold inscription, "To Little from EP." Anita gave away all the gifts Elvis had given her when she married Brewer.

---

4 Last Train to Memphis: The Rise of Elvis Presley © 1994 by Peter Guralnick, Little, Brown & Company (Canada), p. 429.
5 Last Train to Memphis: The Rise of Elvis Presley © 1994 by Peter Guralnick, Little, Brown & Company (Canada), p. 433.

"I kept the guitar for awhile, and then later on I gave it to an old neighbor of mine, Larry Worthy," Anita said. "He said he put it in a museum."

Anita could have made millions of dollars from all of the things Elvis gave her, but she felt it would be wrong and deceptive to profit from him.

Although Presley's family very much supported Elvis' relationship with Anita, not everybody felt the same way. Col. Tom Parker was an ever-present obstacle in the couple's relationship.

"He (Parker) didn't want us to take any pictures. If I was with Elvis and there was a picture made, I was supposed to look down or try to look away," Anita said. "I was not to appear to be too happy, because he

(Parker) didn't want everybody to know our real relationship with each other ... that we really cared for each other." Parker thought if the public knew Presley was in a serious relationship, it might hurt his appeal to his lady fans.

Memories Of Happy Times

Anita recalls many happy, good times at get-togethers with Elvis, his family and friends. "It was just so much fun. We used to sit down and Gladys would fix some kind of greens. She would get some grease and get it really hot on the stove and pour it over the greens. Home cooking. And it was really good. We would go visit his aunts and eat with them, and they were the same kind of people, you know. There were also visits with Patsy, his double cousin. It was a good, close family. I attended a lot of family gatherings at Graceland. They would all come there, and we would go to their houses, too."

"Sometimes just Elvis and I would get on the motorcycle and ride through Memphis. Those were some of my best times with him."

Sometimes Anita and Elvis traveled incognito, riding around Memphis or driving to Tupelo in the old black panel truck Presley had driven when he was a driver for Crown Electric.

"We would get in the truck and Elvis would take me down to Lauderdale Courts, where he used to live when he was poor; he would talk about that a lot, and show me where he came from," Anita said. Presley also drove her to Tupelo to see the simple house where the Presley family had lived before moving to Memphis. "This was all before the Army. After Elvis went into the Army, things were different; everything changed after that."

When Anita, Presley's parents, friends and fans went to the station to see Presley off for the military, he hugged Anita last. "The last thing he said to me was, 'Little, I love you and I will return, and don't forget me.' My heart was being torn away because he was my first love. Elvis was my first love, but Johnny is my true love."

Death Of Gladys Presley

The biggest change in Presley happened after his momma died while he was in the Army, stationed at Fort Hood in Killeen, Texas. The Presley family – Gladys, Vernon, his grandmother, Minnie Mae, a few cousins, and several of Elvis' friends had been living in off-base housing in Killeen; however, in August when Gladys became gravely ill, they went back to Memphis, where she was hospitalized. Presley was granted emergency leave to go home to Memphis, but just a couple of days after he got home, his momma died.

Anita was in New York for an appearance on the Andy Williams Show. Presley called her early that morning and told her the news; she flew to Memphis that night as soon as she finished taping the show.

"When we arrived at Graceland and pulled up in front of the house that night, Elvis and his dad were sitting on the front steps, crying. It was so sad. I got out of the car, and Elvis ran to me saying, 'Little, Little, Little, I've lost her, I've lost her, I've lost her,'" Anita said. Presley wanted her to go inside the house to see Gladys' body which was lying in State in the music room.

"He walked me back, and though there were people all around, I don't remember any of them. I was so upset I didn't see anybody. Elvis walked me directly to the music room and showed me the white coffin which had glass over it. The glass was put over the coffin because Elvis couldn't keep his hands off of his mother. He kept touching her, cradling her in his arms and trying to wake her up. He started talking to her in that baby talk. It was so sad that I just broke down."

A few days after Mrs. Presley was laid to rest, Presley told his friend Klein, "You know, GK, all this Graceland stuff, the movies, the records, it's all been for my mom. It was all for her, and now she can't enjoy it."[6]

Klein observed in his book, "Elvis: My Best Man," that Gladys and Elvis Presley were similar in nature; in addition to sharing the love of a mother and son, they also had a dearly cherished friendship.

---

6 "Elvis: My Best Man," © 2010 by George Klein, Crown Publishing Group, a division of Random House, Inc., New York, NY

"She cared for him so much, and, truly, she was the anchor in his crazy life. He always counted on her for her support, her encouragement, her keen judge of character, and her unconditional love." Klein believes that if Mrs. Presley had lived a full life, Elvis would be with us today.[7]

Soldier Boy

Presley returned to Ft. Hood to complete his training, and then shipped out for two years with the Third Armored Division in Germany. After Presley had been in Germany for less than a week, he called Klein and gave him his mailing address. He asked Klein to send him a box of records every couple of weeks to keep him up to date, and he requested that Klein keep an eye on Anita since she did a noontime radio show at WHHM, the same station where Klein worked as a disc jockey. Presley also asked Klein for the address of a dark-haired girl named Jane Wilbanks. "The fact that Elvis wanted to communicate with her (Jane Wilbanks) was the first indication to me that maybe things weren't as serious with Anita as I'd thought," Klein said.[8]

As far as Anita knew, however, her relationship with Presley was the same as always. He continued to write and call, sending her gifts, and making plans for their future together. An excerpt from a letter Elvis wrote to Anita indicates the seriousness of the relationship:

> *I want you to know that in spite of our being apart I have developed a love for you that cannot be equaled or surpassed by anyone. My every thought is you my darling, every song I hear, every sunset reminds me of the happy and wonderful times we've spent together. I tell you this because I want you to know my feelings ... toward you have not changed, but instead have grown stronger than I ever thought it could. I have hurt you sometimes*

7 "Elvis: My Best Man" © 2010 by George Klein, Crown Publishing Group, a division of Random House, Inc., New York, NY, p. 121-122
8 "Elvis: My Best Man" © 2010 by George Klein, Crown Publishing Group, a division of Random House, Inc., New York, NY, p. 123

because I was mad at some of the things you did or I thought you did, but every time these things happened I thought that maybe you only liked me for what I am, and didn't really love me for myself. These things happen in life baby, misunderstandings, heartbreaks and loneliness, but the fact remains, if it's really love Anita, if we really love each other, it will last... So darling if you still feel the same and if you love me and me alone, we will have a great life together even though you hear things and read things. Just think as you said, everyone knows how I feel about you. I can't explain to you how I crave you and desire your lips...darling. I can feel it now... Remember darling, true love holds its laurels through the ages no matter how loud the clamor of denial. That which deserves to live -- lives. Yours alone, EP

Anita and Elvis often sang and played piano at Graceland. One of their favorite songs, which they referred to as 'their' song, was "I Can't Help It If I'm Still in Love with You." Anita said she and Elvis would sing and play that song for hours.

"When he was in Germany, he sent me a letter telling me 'our' song had changed. Our new song was, 'Please Love Me Forever' by Tommy Edwards," Anita remembered. The song "Soldier Boy" was on the flip side of the record, and Elvis told Anita he was going to record that song. True to his promise, Presley did eventually record that song especially for Anita.

I often perform the song "Soldier Boy" during my Shea Arender Elvis Tribute act, and also for other occasions. When I sing it, I sing it for Anita.

Anita and her daughter walked into my office one day a few years ago, and heard clips I had recorded for a local television '68 Comeback Special remake. When Anita heard my version of "I Can't Help Falling in Love," she couldn't believe it was me. She swore it was Elvis. I said, "Wow! Fooling Anita! I must have officially mastered this craft." I walked with my head held high. Anita smiled and gave me a thumb's up and a wink. All these years and years of hard work had paid off.

Back Home In Memphis

When Presley returned to Memphis in the spring of 1960, after two years of service in Germany, Anita was still part of the scene at Graceland and a big part of Presley's life; however, the feelings he had for the new love in his life, Priscilla Beaulieu, couldn't remain a secret.

Anita learned about Elvis' relationship with Priscilla when she was visiting Elvis in California. She found a letter from Priscilla to Elvis tucked into a book. When he came home from the set that day, she asked him about the letter. Anita said, "I found this letter which says, 'Please call my Dad. I want to come over there and if you call my Dad, I know he will let me come. He will listen to you. I miss you.' So what is this letter? Who is this Priscilla? You said she was just a child? He got so mad because I found the letter."

Anita left that night on a plane for Memphis. When she arrived at Graceland, the telephone was ringing. Presley apologized profusely and insisted that he didn't have a relationship with 14-year-old Priscilla. "He said to me, 'Little, please don't tell anybody about this. This girl is just a child. She's just a 14-year-old child; it means absolutely nothing. She just wants to visit; it means nothing. And if you told anybody, I'd get in a lot of trouble. She's so young.' He just begged me, 'Little, Little, Little.' So I said I wouldn't tell anybody, and I never did."

Anita and Elvis continued to see each other after the letter; however, in early 1962, their relationship ended for good when Anita overheard

Elvis and his daddy, Vernon, talking. "When I was coming down the back stairs into the kitchen at Graceland, I heard Elvis say, 'I'm having the hardest time making up my mind between the two.' Well, I didn't know a lot of things that went on, but I did know that Priscilla had come over and visited. Elvis had talked his way out of that one. I knew she was in his life, but I also knew she was very young. But when I heard him say he was having a hard time making up his mind between the two, I knew exactly what he was talking about. And I had a lot of pride. So I just marched my little self right down the stairs."

Anita said she, Elvis and Vernon sat down in the dining room, and she told Presley she would make the decision for him. "I told him, 'I heard what you said, and I'm leaving.' Then I started crying. After having dating Elvis for five years, we had become very close. The decision to end our relationship was probably the most difficult decision that I've ever made in my life, and when I left, I knew there would be no going back." Anita called her brother and asked him to come to Graceland and get her. She then packed her things and left.

Anita only saw Elvis a few times after the breakup. Once she ran into him in the hallway at the radio station. She spoke to him again later after her marriage to Johnny Brewer in 1964.

The last time Anita saw Elvis was in Las Vegas. "I was walking into the hotel lobby, and I ran into some of Elvis' guys. And they said, 'Why don't you come to the show tonight?'"

So Anita and a lady friend went to the show. They had seats in the reserved section, right in front of the stage. "I never will forget it," Anita said. "Man, he looked so fine up on stage. He was singing right to me. He talked to me; he sang to me. I was just, oh, my goodness!" After the show was over one of the guys approached Anita and told her Elvis would like to see her.

So Anita and her friend went backstage. Elvis and Anita embraced, and the couple went to a private area to sit and talk. They talked for about an hour. During the conversation, Anita said Presley asked her a question.

He said, "I wonder Little, if we made the right decision all those years ago when we decided to split?" Anita said she replied: "Well, of course we made the right decision, because if we hadn't, I wouldn't have my children and you wouldn't have your daughter; that's very important. It was meant to be that we had these children."

Elvis told Anita how much he had missed her. "It was very comforting and reassuring that he still remembered me," Anita said. "I think he still cared, as I did for him. Once you really care for someone, you always care for them in a way."

The last time Anita spoke to Elvis was after Anita's father died. She called to let him know that her father had died and that now she truly knew how it felt to lose a parent. They talked for awhile longer; however, Anita said Elvis didn't sound like himself; his voice was slow and draggy.

Death Of Elvis Presley

Anita learned of Elvis' death when she got a telephone call from a newspaper reporter in Vicksburg, Mississippi where she was living at the time. "The reporter wanted to know my reaction to Elvis' death. I told him that he must be mistaken – it must be Mr. Presley – Vernon – that had died. But he said it was Elvis. I was so surprised – what did he expect? It was terrible. I couldn't believe it. That's how I found out about it. On the telephone. From a stranger. It was a sad, sad day."

Chapter 3

Shea's Friendships with Elvis Contemporaries

Steve Wade
Lighting Technician for Elvis Presley, 1974-1977

"Bullcrap! That's Elvis!" were the first words Steve Wade uttered when he heard me singing Elvis' "American Trilogy" in a small Louisiana recording studio.

Wade, a lighting technician for Elvis Presley, had just walked through the door when he heard the song. He remarked to a fellow musician there, "I remember well when Elvis cut that song." When he was told – that's not Elvis – that's Shea Arender, he simply refused to believe it until he heard me sing and watched me perform.

The friendship that developed from this meeting took Wade, who is also a drummer, on the road with my band, the "C.C. Riders." Playing Elvis Tribute shows with C.C. Riders also caused more than a few instances of déjà vu for Wade.

Wade recalls that many of the stops on our C.C. Riders tour followed the same route that Presley had traveled in the 1950s with the Louisiana Hayride, stopping in small towns where folks were completely Elvis-crazy. He said, "Being backstage with Shea reminded me a lot of being on stage with Elvis. For example, Elvis and Shea both pace around like caged tigers. Before Elvis took the stage, he would have his head sort of cocked to the side, with a look of deep concentration on his face. When Shea was backstage before a show, he did the same exact thing!"

"I remember one show at a theater in rural northeast Louisiana. We were performing a Branson, Missouri-style show with Mickey Gilley's cousin, Gerald Lewis on keyboards. The energy in the place was crazy. Right before we went on, we peeked out the curtains and saw the house was packed – the show was sold out. It was the talk around town and northeast Louisiana, so everybody was there. In the backstage area, the band huddled up for a prayer-like gathering. At that moment when Shea looked over at me, I was in a trance; it felt exactly like being backstage with Elvis. It made the hair rise up on the back of my neck. I couldn't believe that feeling. I still can't. I was speechless."

And Wade is in a position to know what it was like to work with Presley; between 1974 and 1977 he worked as a stagehand and ran spotlights for more than ten Presley shows. Some of his most notable shows in Louisiana were in Alexandria and the Monroe Civic Center. When Wade got the lighting gig for Presley's show, he admitted he was not a fan of Elvis' music. "I wasn't knowledgeable about his music, but once I saw him live, that was it," Wade said, adding that not only did he become a huge fan, but he also became so sentimental about the experience that he still has – and treasures – one of his paycheck stubs from Elvis Presley Enterprises.

As a lighting technician at the Civic Center, Wade had the opportunity to be behind-the-scenes with many big acts such as the Beach Boys, Chicago and Grand Funk Railroad. But none of those shows electrified

Wade like Presley's show did. "Not only was Presley's performance bigger than life, but also his stage show – and his effect on the audience – was unbelievable," Wade said.

There were twelve spotlights for Presley's show – all huge lights called "Super-Troopers." Wade explained, "The lights are harder to run than a TV antenna. The light is created by two welding rods creating an arc, but not touching; the light bounces off a reflector to make an intensely bright light. It was a challenge to keep the rods at exactly the right spacing – not touching, but close enough to create the light. Super-Troopers are longer than a Cadillac and bigger around than a drainage ditch – three feet in circumference."

Wade continued, "Not only were twelve huge spotlights running throughout the show, but seven ambulance services were also running overtime, carrying away women that were passing out right and left. They hauled them out as quickly as the ambulances could make a run to the hospital and get back to the civic center."

In 2007 Wade received a call from a friend in Bastrop, Louisiana saying he was in the studio to do some Elvis recording and needed a drummer. Would Wade be interested? Yes, he was very interested in the gig. He grabbed his stick bag and hit the road, burning up the twenty-two miles between Monroe and Bastrop.

That's when he met me. He was amused because I couldn't stand still during a recording. He would say, "Dude, we're not playing live. Why are you gyrating in the studio?" Working with me brought back so many memories of working with Elvis. Once Wade remarked, "I was in the drum room about to die. I was over there squalling because Shea couldn't stand still."

When Wade and I first started working together, we instantly developed a chemistry, and a sort of shorthand communication. Both of us were

35

intimately familiar with Presley's arrangements of his songs – through all of Elvis' era and incarnations – which was a tremendous benefit both for live shows and in the studio. For example, if I said something like: "Let's open like Elvis did in the '68 comeback special, then fuse it with a 1973 Aloha show," Wade would know precisely what I wanted him to do.

Wade also knew how to set up and run the lights for specific Elvis eras, which further enhanced the authenticity of my tribute shows. He said, "We did the shows similar to the way Elvis did – just on a smaller scale – for venues of 500 to 3500. Arender was always very active in the production of the shows due to his extensive knowledge of Elvis' production style."

Wade was continually awed by the similarities between Elvis and me. He would remark, "He is Elvis made over. It's like he has permission to do this. If Elvis were here, he would give his blessing to the show. I guarantee that he'd say, 'I can't do it anymore, but you can. Get after it boy, and do your best.' I've seen a lot of impersonators and tribute artists – a lot of them – and none of them comes close to Shea."

Hanging With the Memphis Mafia

Although Wade didn't have much direct interaction with Presley, he was involved – beyond the shows – with Elvis' band and entourage. He recalled one embarrassing encounter with Elvis.

"I took the Memphis Mafia members out many times after the shows, taking them around Monroe, Louisiana. I even remember one time in particular that the guys wanted to go out for ice cream. As the Mafia guys and I were preparing to leave the hotel, I came face-to-face with Presley in kind of an embarrassing way. We were making a pretty good amount of noise; in fact, we made enough racket to cause Elvis to peek out of his room to see what everybody was doing. He was trying to sleep, and we were hootin' and hollerin' and making all kinds of noise! But Elvis was real nice about being disturbed. What an experience, getting to hang out with the Memphis Mafia and being a part of Elvis' shows. I have truly been blessed."

Mickey Gilley
Country music legend

You may be thinking, "What does Mickey Gilley have to do with Elvis?"

I first saw Mickey Gilley in 2006 at a concert at his theater in Branson. A year later I traveled and played with Mickey's cousin, Gerald Lewis for a six month Gospel special called, "The Elvis Gospel Experience with Shea Arender and Gerald Lewis." Although I had been an admirer and a student of Mickey Gilley's music for many years, I listened to more of his music during the time I spent touring with Gerald. The information Gerald shared about his cousin made me want to meet him personally.

The opportunity for a meeting presented itself in the summer of 2009 when I learned that Mickey was going to perform at a big homecoming concert in his hometown of Ferriday, Louisiana. I drove into town and spent much of the day helping Gilley's family with concert preparations.

The town had also erected a statue in the town square in honor of Gilley's musical accomplishments and contributions to his hometown.

I was backstage when Gilley first saw me walking up the stairs and told his cousins, "I have met a lot of people in this world and names and faces slip my mind, but I know this guy from somewhere. There is something different about him," so I walked over, greeted him and told him I was really looking forward to his performance. He said it was nice to meet me, but he was preoccupied with making sure the sound was right for the evening performance.

A little later, one of Mickey's family members, William Atkins said, "You should hear this guy sing an Elvis song!"

Mickey immediately responded, "Elvis is the King! My cousin, Jerry Lee Lewis and I used to have friendly debates about that. Jerry always wanted to compete with Elvis a bit, and because he and Elvis were both former Sun Records recording artists, there was always a little friendly competition between them."

Later that afternoon we all went to lunch together and discussed how music has changed through the years. An aspiring singer or musician can't get to the top of the music chain as easily as in times past. In those days, getting your song on radio would ensure your success, but now everything is Clear Channel or regional. What may be popular in one area of the country may not even receive air-play in another part of the country.

After lunch, we went back to the theater and Mickey said to me, "Son, you look like Elvis; can you sing like him?"

I immediately began singing several Elvis songs. He listened, then joined in, as we sang them together. Next, I began singing one of Mickey's songs, "I'm Just a Fool For You Baby." Mickey was pleased that I not only knew Elvis' music, but was also familiar with his music as well. I mentioned the song, "You Don't Know Me," which had been recorded by Elvis and Ray Charles and later by Mickey; I told him that I really wanted to hear him sing it. Although that song wasn't on the program,

Mickey added it and told the audience what an honor it had been for him to record a song made famous by Elvis and Ray Charles.

After the show I had a chance to visit a little longer with Mickey. He never could remember my name, Shea. He kept calling me Elvis and telling others that "Elvis" was in the house. He told me how much he had admired Elvis and what an influence Elvis had been on his own musical career.

Before I left, he invited me to come to Branson when he was performing, and sing with him. Unfortunately, he had an accident shortly afterward which disabled him and reduced his ability to perform for a time. He has returned to the stage now, but the use of his hands is limited. Although I never had the opportunity to sing with Mickey on stage, I will always consider it an honor that he asked me to do it.

Gene Shaw
Godfather of Elvis Tributes

Gene Shaw - a Solo Artist as well as a Tribute Artist. As a great ambassador of goodwill, he has achieved the distinction of performing Elvis Tribute shows for over forty-five years. He received Vernon Presley's (Elvis' father) blessing for his performances back in early 1978, and his performance in 500 Elvis Tribute Shows one year earned him recognition in the Guinness Book of World Records for the most Elvis Tribute Shows in a single year. The first riffs of an Elvis song were heard on the streets of Monroe, Louisiana in the mid-1950s, and Gene still manages to perform a few shows here in the 2000s. He is known in this large community of tributes as the Godfather because he has dedicated his whole life to the stage as a means of helping others and giving honor to the artist he portrays.

Throughout his career he has devoted his time to helping young artists learn strategies for being successful Tribute Artists. I have been the recipient of his help many times throughout my career. I worked very hard once to win a world Elvis Tribute competition (long before Elvis Presley Enterprises sanctioned these contests). After winning, I was burned out on the whole Elvis Tribute routine. Gene gave me some fresh ideas to kick-start a new series of shows. Then he helped me get some new suits and learn some new songs. He has taken a lot of talented people with no connection to the craft and loaned them suits and music, and helped guide them along to a successful career.

His list of credits and musical experiences is quite impressive. He was flown to New York once to sing with the Jordanaires and has sung on stage with great performers like the Platters and Tony Orlando, to name a few. He has also hosted many Elvis Tribute Artist contests. Although he has released an Elvis-influenced Gospel album, he remains Gene Shaw. He says, "I didn't try to sound like Elvis; I just sang the songs from the heart to God."

Gene Shaw with Jordanaires in New York 1995

After Elvis' death in 1977, it was crazy in Memphis. Media reporters and tabloid photographers were hanging around Graceland and other parts of the city hoping to get a good story or picture for their news agencies. Shaw, a friend of Elvis' family, went to Memphis to visit Vernon. Due to his strong resemblance to Elvis, one of the photographers shot some pictures of him and published them with the headline, "Elvis is still alive!!!!" Gene said, "I was shocked to have all of this happen. I was just going to Memphis to visit and pay my respects."

Shaw's connection with Elvis grew after he met Mike McGregor in the late 1980s. Not much has been written about McGregor, but he played a huge role in Elvis' success. Originally from Oxford, MS, he lived at Graceland for eight years. He created much of Elvis' turquoise jewelry and made his tour jackets. He took care of Elvis' horses, did all of his saddle work, and did other maintenance around the ranch. McGregor became a good friend of Shaw, and they enjoyed getting together and sharing their memories of Elvis with each other.

There were many sad days in Memphis during the late 1970s. Gene remembers the family's frustration over Elvis fans slipping around his grave and being caught trying to dig it up. Elvis was originally laid to rest at Forest Hill Cemetery in Memphis, but was later moved to the Meditation Gardens in the back yard of Graceland. The interesting thing is that many credible sources have said that Elvis' body was not laid to rest in the place noted by the marker in the back yard. Instead, the family actually buried him under the Angel Monument at Graceland to prevent the grave from being disturbed. Wow, what a crazy world!

Gene and I have shared many of our experiences of performing Elvis Tribute Shows. Most every year, he and I perform for a cancer benefit concert that is usually live on local Television in Gene's home town of Monroe, Louisiana. We raise a minimum of $70,000 every year for the desperate needs of these kids. This one live concert helps hundreds of kids with cancer and funds all of their projects for the whole year. We do not accept any proceeds from the concert; all the money goes to the kids.

When Gene and I perform a joint concert, he usually does a portrayal of the late Elvis in the 1975-77 era. I do the 1968 comeback or do the early 1970s; occasionally I do the 1950s rockabilly tunes. All in all, my friendship with Gene Shaw has been a blessing to me personally and to my career as a Tribute Artist. His passion for keeping the memory of Elvis alive is heartfelt and authentic. His knowledge and commitment has been second to none and continues to motivate and bless people with talent even today after being on the job over forty-five years.

Shea with Gene Shaw in a live TV concert (seen by over 50,000 viewers.)

May God Bless Gene Shaw for paving the way for the younger Tribute Artists and for keeping the music alive.

Wayne Carman
Elvis' Friend and Karate Training Partner[1]

Wayne's connection with Elvis began in December 1970 when he received a phone call from Red West who was chief of Elvis' security. Red requested some training in the use of nunchakus for Elvis' security staff.

Several months of instruction with Red went by before Wayne received an invitation to meet Elvis one evening at the Memphian Theatre. He was ushered to a seat directly behind Elvis. His image of Elvis as some sort of superhuman being with no connection to common, ordinary people was destroyed in short order that evening. Elvis laughed and interacted with those around him, ate popcorn and drank Pepsi just like any ordinary person.

During intermission Wayne and Elvis discussed the martial arts. Elvis had been in martial arts training since his Army days, and Wayne invited Elvis to visit Kang Rhee's martial arts school in Memphis and work out with him.

After the movie, Elvis invited Wayne to get his car and follow Elvis' entourage as they cruised around Memphis. Wayne said he felt like he was with a bunch of high school kids as they cruised around town in the wee hours, stopping every now and then to talk, then getting back in their cars and cruising some more. Wayne has referred to that initial meeting in his book as "Reel Time With a Legend."

That evening initiated a friendship and partnership between Wayne and Elvis that endured until Elvis' death in 1977.

---

1 Information and photos taken from Wayne's book, "Elvis' Karate Legacy" and used with permission. For more information on Wayne Carman's book, please contact Legacy Entertainment, Inc. by emailing carmantcb1@tri-lakes.net.

Several months went by before Elvis was able to schedule time to attend one of Wayne's classes at the school. Elvis was impressed with Kang Rhee's abilities and the different style from the way he had been trained, so he began attending classes there. He had a deep desire to excel in areas other than the entertainment field. His skill in martial arts earned him great respect from the other students.

Often Elvis' work-out intensity brought hilarious moments to the class. On one occasion, the question was asked, "What would you do if someone was standing ten feet away from you with a gun pulled?"

Elvis quickly stood, straightened his uniform, then knelt and put his hands together. The class remained silent until someone finally asked what he was doing. With a big smile Elvis replied, "When someone is standing ten feet away with a drawn gun, that's when you pray!" The class broke out in laughter.

Elvis dreamed of opening schools for instruction of the martial arts. His martial arts philosophy involved uniting several karate styles, while adding a foundation of respect along with his own T.C.B. (Taking Care of Business) principles. His three principles of T.C.B. were:

1) Have faith in God.
2) Always be positive, think positive and act positive.
3) Never give up!

Wayne has personally used and taught many of Elvis' principles through the years. He said that Elvis had never been given enough credit for his wisdom.

There is no other book on the market that describes in depth the spiritual aspect of Elvis' life as does Wayne's book, "Elvis' Karate Legacy." God was one of the most important things in Elvis' life. I was very pleased to read Wayne's book and also to have him share with me personally many

45

of his fond memories on this subject. It not only made a difference in people's lives back then, but the discussion in this book of the spiritual development of the heart, mind and soul is also making a difference in people's lives today. This book is a must-have for Elvis and Martial Arts fans.

My first meeting with Wayne Carman was in Branson, Missouri at the conclusion of one of my Elvis Tribute shows. He was very pleased with what he saw, and felt I had done justice to Elvis' name and legacy. That initial meeting started a friendship that continues to this day.

The first time I called him, I said, "This is Shea Arender," and he said, "Who?" I said, "Shea Arender, the guy you saw in the concert in Branson; the Real Deal." From that point forward he began calling me "The Real Deal," and that is how he addresses me every time we talk.

I've done some research into the meaning of my nickname and believe it acknowledges my accuracy in portrayal of Elvis as well as my persistence and consistence in setting goals and getting things done.

Through the years our friendship has deepened as I have shared memories of Anita and her stories about Elvis, and life on the road as Elvis. Wayne has shared memories of Elvis' devotion to God and the spiritual experiences they shared together, as well as Elvis' dreams for helping others and making a difference in the world.

Handwritten Note from Elvis to God:

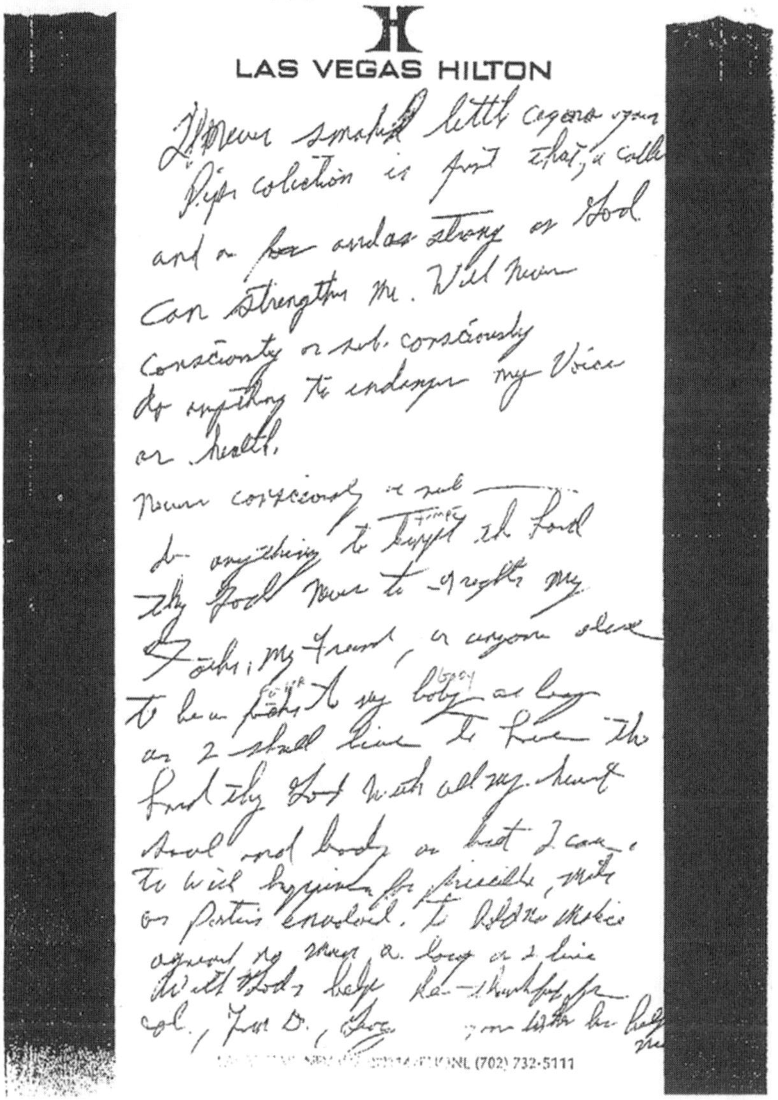

Handwritten Note from Elvis to God:

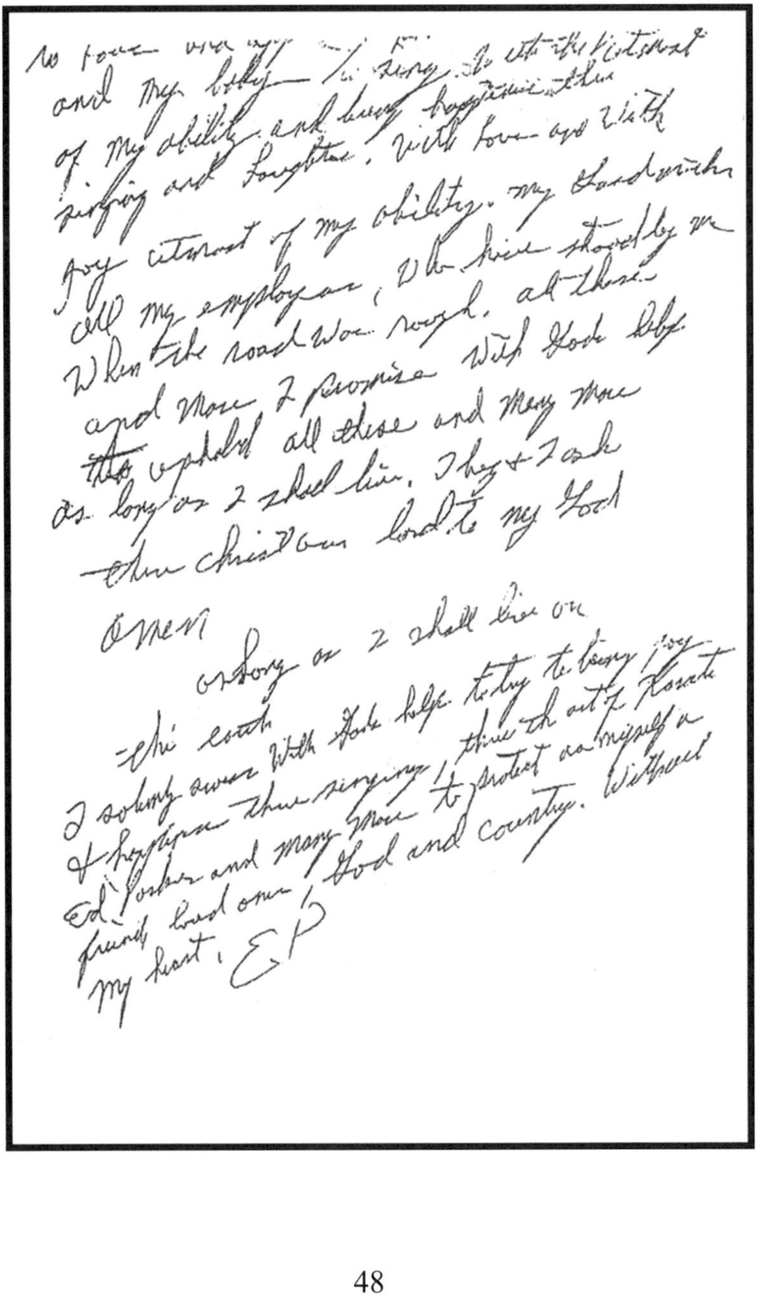

to [illegible] [illegible] [illegible] [illegible] to [illegible] the [illegible]
and my [illegible] to sing. [illegible] [illegible] [illegible]
of my ability and bring happiness [illegible]
singing and laughter. With love and With
joy [illegible] of my ability. my [illegible]
All my employees, Who have stood by me
When the road was rough. all these
and more I promise With Gods help
to uphold all these and many more
as long as I shall live. Thy [illegible] I ask
[illegible] Christ our lord to my God

amen

as long as I shall live on
this earth
I solemnly swear With Gods help to try to bring joy
& happiness thru singing, thru the art of Karate
and many more to protect [illegible] myself [illegible]
friend [illegible] God and country. Without
my heart, EP

Partial Transcriptions of Handwritten Notes from Elvis to God:

I'll never smoke little cigars again. Pipe collection is just that, a collection and for as strong as God can strengthen me, will never consciously or sub-consciously do anything to endanger my voice or health. Never consciously or not do anything to upset the Lord thy God. Never to (?) my Father, my friend, or anyone else to be a friend to my body as long as I shall live. To love the Lord thy God with all my heart, soul and body or best as I can. To wish happiness for Priscilla, Mike, or parties involved. To hold no malice against no man as long as I live. With God's help be thankful for Col. Tom P., George, everyone who has helped me and will help me.

To love and appreciate Linda with all my heart, and my body. To sing with the utmost of my ability and bring happiness thru singing and laughter. With love and with joy utmost of my ability. My Grandmother, all my employees, who have stood by me when the road was rough. All these and more I promise with God's help to uphold all these and many more as long as I shall live. They and I ask thru Christ our Lord to my God. Amen.

As long as I shall live on this earth I solemnly swear with God's help to try to bring joy and happiness thru singing, thru the art of Karate, Ed Parker and many more, to protect as myself a friend, loved one, God and country. With all my heart. E. P.

Elvis patting Wayne Carman on the back – like a "That-A-Boy" award!

Photo - Courtesy of Elvis' Karate Legacy by Wayne Carman

Elvis takes a blow from Red West and displays the use of his karate power in not allowing the blow to hurt.

Photo - Courtesy of Elvis' Karate Legacy by Wayne Carman

Elvis prepares to use finger techniques to Red's face.

An unbelievable demonstration by Elvis – allowing Red to put his fist in his throat while Elvis pushed him back.

Photo - Courtesy of Elvis' Karate Legacy by Wayne Carman

Elvis wanted the world to know martial arts could help ordinary people do extraordinary things. Elvis discovered this and wanted to share it with the world.

Elvis said that having a rank test was like a woman having a baby – something one never forgets. Here Elvis hits a student to highlight the student rank test.

Photo - Courtesy of Elvis' Karate Legacy by Wayne Carman

53

Pictured above is Elvis' creation of the T.C.B. patch with seven stars representing God's perfect number. Elvis designed the patch, and Kang Rhee had it made for him. The words... Faith, Spirit, and Discipline on the patch show his method of Taking Care of Business. With the color black representing the heavens, white representing purity and red representing the blood of Jesus, the patch was one of the contributions Elvis made to the martial arts.

Photo - Courtesy of Elvis' Karate Legacy by Wayne Carman

The ring displayed above was a reproduction Wayne Carman had made for himself. The original ring bearing the T.C.B. logo was Elvis' favorite and is now on display at Graceland.

Shea with Wayne Carman in Branson, Missouri, 2010.

Chapter 4

A Tribute to Elvis

Formula For Success

I believe the formula for being a successful Elvis Tribute Artist has to be embedded within you to begin with. You must have a passion for Elvis' music, his movies, his historical concerts – you just need to really know as much as possible about Elvis Presley. However, it was a lot different for me because of my background. I am a Southern American, from the same area that Elvis was from. I grew up just knowing about Elvis Presley – he was always a part of my life, so it was different for me than for other artists.

- IMMERSE YOURSELF IN ELVIS PRESLEY'S MUSIC: Somebody starting out should immerse themselves completely in all of Elvis' music. They should pick out about 50 to 100 songs that they like, and get really familiar with the lyrics and vocal progression in the songs.

- VOCAL STYLE IS EVERYTHING: To be a very good Elvis Tribute Artist, you take the song -- for example, maybe a song recorded in 1956. Then sing it in the same vocal style – the way Elvis sounded – in 1956. You can't use the same vocal application for a 1970s song as you use for a 1950s song. Elvis' voice changed in his different eras.

- IF YOU CAN'T HIT THE HIGH NOTES, DON'T LOWER THE PITCH - CUT THE SONG: Elvis' voice was so powerful that the dynamics were intensified by the high notes he sang. Because no one can be Elvis, a good Tribute Artist needs to be able to hit the high notes in order to recreate the same powerful dynamics that Elvis did. If you lower the pitch on the song, you lose the dynamic intensity, and fail to achieve the effect that made Elvis' performances so powerful.

- LEARN THE MOVES: Some Tribute Artists and impersonators will take Elvis' moves from Jailhouse Rock and add them to a 1970s application. Elvis didn't move in the 1970s like he did in the 50s. In the jumpsuit era, his gyrations and Elvis-the-pelvis hip thrusts were performed in a more stationary manner. He performed more of a hip thrust shuffle in 1954-60. He developed a more conservative performance style after that. You can't use the same application for all the eras.

When people tell me, "you don't really move like him, or you're not doing those pelvis thrusts like Elvis," it is my job as a Tribute Artist to educate them concerning the different moves that accompanied the different musical styles for each era of Elvis' life. When he came back to the stage after his stint in the Army, he moved differently. The pelvic thrust moves were replaced with Karate stance routines and dances during Elvis' jumpsuit era. The jumpsuits he wore were patterned after karate-style workout clothing.

- YOU'VE GOT TO KNOW THE RULES TO BREAK 'EM. Once you have mastered and precisely replicated Elvis' vocals and his moves, you can develop your own style with the Elvis act. For example, I have incorporated the Elvis songs "Blue Moon," "A Little Less Conversation," and several movie hits from the 60s into my shows, although there is no record that Elvis ever performed these particular songs in live shows. I just inform the audience that although Elvis didn't do these songs as part of a certain era, I want to do them with my own interpretation of how he might have performed them. Sometimes my shows have extra horn or guitar solos that weren't in Elvis' original recordings. But I always make sure to keep the songs as stylistically and vocally accurate as possible. A serious Tribute Artist will create his own arrangements in keeping with the vocal and stylistic performances of the original artist, whereas an impersonator will simply copy the original arrangements of the one he is impersonating.

Elvis vs. Elvis-ish

The Merriam-Webster dictionary defines an impersonator as one who "assumes or acts in the character of;" in other words, someone who imitates or acts like a character.

Merriam-Webster defines "tribute" as "a gift or service showing respect, gratitude or affection;" or that "indicates the worth, virtue or effectiveness of the one in question, such as 'the design is a tribute to his ingenuity.'"

I am a Tribute Artist. I accurately and precisely pay tribute to Elvis with my performances. My hair is my own, not a Halloween-type fake wig and sideburns. I don't lip-synch. My costumes are authentic replicas, not poorly rendered fakes. I portray Elvis accurately through all of his eras. My show productions are pretty close to Elvis' shows. If I vary from the original or do something that Elvis didn't do, I usually tell the audience that is what I'm doing.

Elvis imitators were around, even when Elvis was alive. Elvis impersonators started cropping up like weeds in the springtime after Elvis died. However, there were very few who did a mainstream tribute show. In 1977, the term "imitator" became "impersonator" when used to describe Elvis-ish acts. Most impersonators – other than a select few – didn't have the full package. Most costumes were inaccurate, and the shows were watered down. Still, most could not pull it off, despite the fact that they were making $50,000 a week doing Las Vegas shows in the years shortly after Elvis died!

Elvis acts started using the term "Tribute Artist" in the 1990s, to distinguish more authentic acts from the impersonators. However, many who used the term "Tribute Artist" were actually "impersonators" – they just used a new term to describe what they were doing. Many people don't know the difference between the two. However, there are many differences.

True Tribute Artists strive to present a more authentic show. They focus on the artist performing the tribute – paying tribute to Elvis through their learned interpretation of Presley's onstage mastery.

Elvis Impressionists – These are people who add Elvis songs to their set list and try to imitate Elvis' mannerisms, looks or vocals during their performance. If done in good taste, it can be impressive to see. However, many of them are making more of a mockery of the song than giving honorary tribute to Elvis.

Impersonators -- a lot of them -- think they are Elvis. Many impersonators are actually imposters. They put on a fake accent and assume a fake persona, on- and off-stage. How can you consistently fake a Southern American accent if you are not from Southern United States?

For example, I am a true fan of Pavarotti. I studied opera when I was in Italy. I learned to sing in Italian. However, even though I sang in Italian, I am not a native Italian. The Italians who heard me sing one afternoon at a café outside of Venice thought I did a good job singing in Italian. However, later that night there was a large man who sort of looked like Pavarotti who asked me if I knew what those words I was singing meant. Although I had studied Italian, I didn't really understand the message of my song. I didn't know what it was like to grow up in Rome during hard times. Even though my vocal performance was good, it just wasn't the same. When you are an Elvis Tribute Artist, I believe you aren't just playing a role – you are representing Elvis' heritage – you are representing the South USA and Southern music roots.

Perhaps I come across as a little conceited with all the information I have presented, but the Elvis Tribute world is supposed to be a brotherhood. Consequently, it can be a cut-throat and very competitive market, and one must distinguish the difference between a true tribute and a recreationalist.

I think it's great that there are many millions of Elvis fans worldwide, and thousands of impersonators try to bring Elvis to life on stage. However, I don't think an impersonator who is a native of another country can truly bring an accurate Elvis show to the stage. An American audience will most likely be able to tell the difference.

Being a Tribute Artist – or even a decent impersonator – is much more than doing a Karaoke performance of an Elvis song, but some don't know the difference or may not even care. Many impersonators are coming from a non-foundational Elvis background, with little or no vocal training and they're trying to be a mainstream Elvis act. It just doesn't work.

I would advise all Elvis Tribute Artists to visit Mississippi and the Memphis area and learn the culture of the areas and everything they can about Elvis before attempting to perform an Elvis act. People will have questions concerning Elvis, his music and the places he lived, and if the artist isn't educated about those subjects, he will look foolish to his fans. You need to study the Blues and Gospel music, and then you still might not be able to pull it off. I believe you need to have the proper musical foundation in Blues, Gospel, and Rockabilly in order to be a good, accurate Elvis Tribute Artist.

The same goes for female Elvis impersonators. Elvis was a man; therefore, a female cannot appropriately impersonate his style of performing. If Elvis was alive and he could choose anybody to pay proper tribute to him – I think he'd chose a Caucasian, Southern American male – preferably from Mississippi or Tennessee. On the other hand, I believe it is flattering to see women who appreciate Elvis' music and include his songs as part of their personal concert repertoire.

When you're bringing Elvis to people – especially people whose only Elvis experience is seeing a Tribute Artist's performance as Elvis – it is important to be as accurate and respectful as possible. It is important to portray the King from your perspective. You can add your own personal elements to the show – in moderation. But those variances need to be carefully noted.

Ask yourself: Would Elvis like it? Would Elvis have done that? A lot of people just scratch the surface in their portrayal of Elvis – it is important not to confuse an impersonator or Tribute Artist with a huge fan.

I've always thought Elvis Tribute Artist contests were a little comical, since well over half of the impersonators would be more qualified to perform in a Karaoke show. The contests were called Tribute Artist contests when in reality they were impersonator contests. The result is a tenuous balance between Tribute Artist individuality versus impersonator mimicry. Perhaps this explains why I dropped off the competitive Elvis impersonator circuit after winning the world championship. I don't relish performing as one Elvis among many. It's more watered down than individualism. If one of those acts was to come to South Mississippi, they would no doubt be embarrassed by getting booed off the stage. I never really enjoyed participating in those contests anyway because the judges would penalize our performance for very unimportant details that made no difference to the audience.

The Importance Of Authenticity

I strive to portray Elvis as accurately as I can. I own custom-made costumes, very expensive, exact replicas of Elvis' costumes such as The White Lion and the Black Matador jumpsuit costumes which were originally crafted in the early 1970s. I have an authentic 1968 Comeback Special costume, as well as a gold lamé costume and several others.

A lot of Tribute Artists aren't wearing authentic costumes. They are wearing cheap fabric costumes. I have mine custom made in a similar fabric to the fabric used in Elvis' original costumes. I probably have spent over $20,000 throughout my career as an Elvis Tribute Artist on my authentic costumes.

And I also have both replica and real jewelry the same as Elvis wore in concert, such as the TCB logo on a chain, rings and other accessories. In all I do when being Elvis, I have dedicated myself to doing it right, with proper respect.

To conclude this chapter, I submit a story and short note from Elvis concerning his opinion on the qualifications of a good Tribute Artist.

The story is told that a tribute performer sent a packet of performance ideas to Elvis, and an Elvis staff member reviewed it before bringing it to Elvis' attention. Elvis responded with a short note to the performer. I believe his words could apply to any tribute show performance.

Elvis' 1977 Letter to Tribute Performers

I really do appreciate you, a fan... and mimicry is a sincere form of being a fan. Do develop your own special talents and abilities also.

This is a great compliment to me that you would work so hard on this act like mine, but never neglect your own talent to be yourself. You can take my influence and put your own into it.

Best wishes in the future and God bless you

Elvis Presley

Chapter 5

Elvis Guitars

This chapter contains a list of Elvis' performance guitars from the very beginning of his career to the end. I realize that the quality of some of these photos is not that great, but you will get an idea of what each guitar looked like. Many of these photos are very old and hard to find. Each photo contains a description name of the guitar and the year or years he played it.

Elvis Presley Backstage 1954   Martin 000-18 1954

Martin D-18   1954-55   Martin D-28   1955-56

1956 Gibson J200   1956-70

1960 Gibson J200   1960-68   1968 Hagstrom Viking   1968

1963 Gibson Super 400   1968

Elvis borrowed this guitar. His original had a
different pick guard.

1964 Gretsch Country Gentleman   1970

1968 Gibson Ebony J200   1974-75

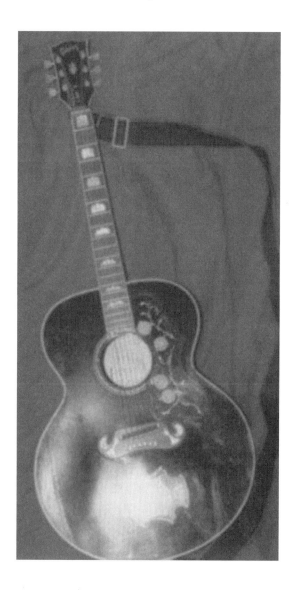

1969 Gibson Ebony Dove   1971-73, briefly in 1975

1970's Gibson Dove Custom   1975-76

1974 Guild F-50   1976   1976 Martin D-35   1976-77

1970's Martin D-28   1977

Chapter 6

Blues History and Influence on Elvis

"The origins of Blues is not unlike the origins of life. For many years it was recorded only by memory, and relayed only live, and in person. The Blues were born in the North Mississippi Delta following the Civil War. Influenced by African roots, field hollers, ballads, church music and rhythmic dance tunes called jump-ups evolved into a style of music for a singer who would engage in call-and-response with his guitar. He would sing a line, and the guitar would answer."

"The Blues... its 12-bar, bent-note melody is the anthem of a race, bonding itself together with cries of shared self-victimization. Bad luck and trouble are always present in the Blues, and always the result of others, pressing upon unfortunate and downtrodden poor souls, yearning to be free from life's troubles. Relentless rhythms repeat the chants of sorrow, and the pity of a lost soul many times over. This is the Blues."

"Arthur "Big Boy" Crudup, Wyonnie Harris, and Big Mama Thornton wrote and performed the songs that would make a young Elvis Presley world renowned."[1]

---

1   http://www.history-of-rock.com/blues.htm

There were two areas of the United States that were noted for their Blues music, and each had its own distinction.

The Delta Blues originated in the Mississippi Delta, a region of the United States that stretches from Memphis, Tennessee in the north to Vicksburg, Mississippi in the south, and the Mississippi River on the west to the Yazoo River on the east. The dominant instruments used are guitar, harmonica and cigar box guitar, with slide guitar (usually on the steel guitar) being a hallmark of the style. The vocal styles range from introspective and soulful to passionate and fiery.

The Chicago Blues developed when ex-slaves migrated from the agricultural South to the industrial cities of the North. They took the acoustic Delta Blues music and made it louder through the use of amplifiers and microphones. Other instruments such as piano, drums, saxophone and trumpet were added. The style was also expanded beyond the traditional six-note Blues scale by adding other notes from the major scale as well as dominant ninth chords, thus giving the music more of a "Jazz" feel.[2]

Since Elvis grew up in Tupelo, Mississippi and Memphis, Tennessee, he was more influenced by the heartfelt emotion and personal expression that was so prevalent in the Delta Blues music.

The Southern states welcomed a variety of musical genres including Rockabilly, Country, Gospel and Blues. Often the styles were blended together. The racial issues that divided the South were often put aside in the 1950s in many of the music clubs that featured Black Rhythm and Blues. These predominantly black clubs began opening up to white youth, and the talents of black and white musicians and singers was utilized.

In the early 1900s, Beale Street in Memphis, Tennessee, was filled with clubs, restaurants and shops, many of which were owned by African-

2 Wikipedia Encyclopedia – Chicago Blues; Delta Blues

Americans. It was an area where black people could go to socialize, and sing and play their music without being intimidated by whites.[3] Here was an area where one could escape from prejudice and be judged on talent alone.

From the 1920s to the 1940s, many Blues and Jazz legends such as Louis Armstrong, Muddy Waters, Albert King, Memphis Minnie, B. B. King, Rufus Thomas, and Rosco Gordon played on Beale Street and helped develop the style known as Memphis Blues. B.B. King was billed as "the Beale Street Blues Boy."[4] Many stories are told of a young Elvis frequenting the music clubs of Beale Street to listen to such Blues greats as B. B. King, Little Junior Parker and Rufus Thomas.

When World War II brought many young soldiers to Memphis, Mayor Crump closed Beale Street to protect them from the gambling, prostitution and cocaine trades. As the clubs began to close their doors, many of Memphis' best Blues artists left the city and migrated to Chicago, where the Delta Blues acoustic style changed and became electrified.[5]

Elvis was influenced by the Blues as a music genre. He admired many of the Blues greats to the extent that he recorded many of their songs. However, traces of their music, delivery and style were also evident in many of his other recordings.

Elvis' singles recorded on the "Sun" label consisted of a Blues side and a Country side. "That's All Right, Mama," "Mystery Train," and "Good Rockin' Tonight" were examples of the Blues influence. This was of course consistent with the frequently reported comment by Sam Phillips that he was looking for a white boy with "the Negro sound and the Negro feel."

---

3 Memphis Elvis Style, Cindy Hazen and Mike Freeman (1997)
4 Wikipedia Encyclopedia – Beale Street
5 http://www.history-of-rock.com/blues.htm

Joe Cocker, one of the finest white Blues singers the world has ever known, once stated that Elvis was the greatest white Blues singer in the world.

Elvis' Blues influence is dramatically apparent by the ongoing accusation that he was 'the white boy who stole the Blues.' In reality, Elvis took characteristics of the various musical genres that influenced him and blended them together, forming a catalyst for transforming "a mainstream popular music scene dominated by the white-bread sounds of Perry Como and Frank Sinatra into a more integrated and diverse beast than it had ever been before."[6]

Blues Influence on a Mississippi/Louisiana Boy

Welcome to the Mississippi Delta, the birthplace of much American music. The Delta is strongly associated with the origins of several genres of popular music, including the Delta Blues, Jazz, and Rock 'n Roll. The music was born from the struggles of many sharecroppers and tenant farmers, for which poverty and hardship were ever present. Statistically, Mississippi may be one of the poorest states in the United States, but it is by far one of the richest in music culture and development. Its Blues roots date far back to the early 1820s when the African slaves were brought over to America for agricultural work, although the exact origin of the Blues is still unknown. The first recognizable Blues music originated during the Civil War era. The slaves on Mississippi plantations in the early 1860s produced some of the first riffs of Blues tunes.

My Blues journey has always been a big part of my career and influence. Although I was born in Mississippi, I spent my school years in Louisiana; then at age eighteen I returned to my native state to attend college and become more immersed in learning about the rich musical culture of the Mississippi Delta.

6 Elvis After Elvis: The Posthumous Career of A Living Legend, Gilbert B. Rodman (1996)

Some of the famous names that have influenced me on my Mississippi Blues Journey are McKinley Morganfield (more commonly known as Muddy Waters), BB King, Robert Johnson, and Arthur "Big Boy" Crudup, (writer of "That's All Right Mama"). But the greatest influence on my musical education and career was, by far, Elvis Presley. I was drawn to the Blues, and the rhythm of Elvis' music. The melody and words of the songs spoke to the hardships in life that exist around the world. The rhythms of the music would loosen the hardships of life and give me hope of a brighter tomorrow.

The Delta has always been a place of much mystery and mystique. The intense passion and melody produced by the voices of that area fascinated me. You could drive through most any small community in the Delta and find poor, older black men sitting on their porches, telling their life story with a beat-up guitar and occasionally a harmonica.

One of my most interesting journeys occurred in the summer of 2006 when I was scheduled to play at some Blues events deep in the Mississippi Delta. On the way to my concert, I decided to stop off in Rolling Fork, Mississippi. It was a steamy, hot summer day in which you could see steam rising from these poor streets like a puff of smoke. As I got out of my car and looked around, the old buildings, the rustic Civil War

Muddy Waters, known as the "Hoochie-Coochie Man"

graves, and the cotton boles that traced the streets took me back in time to the 1930s and 40s.

I walked down the street and began asking if anyone knew some Blues music. At first they thought I was a foreigner, but as soon as I opened my mouth, they immediately recognized my native accent. One elderly man looked at me and said, "The Blues? You want the Blues? Well, we are the Blues." He pointed in the direction of a house where several men were sitting on the porch. They noticed me walking toward them, and in a loud excited voice, one of them said, "Oh my!! I'm seeing things today. There's Elvis!!"

I looked around, thinking they could not possibly see what I looked like from that distance. My curiosity was aroused, and my mind began to race as I walked toward them. I sensed something special and different about this place and these people, and immediately began singing some old Blues tunes in my head. The guy who had told me that he and his friends were the Blues suddenly disappeared. He must have run away quickly, or perhaps never started walking with me to begin with.

The first thing I said was, "Hey y'all, what's goin' on?" They all responded at the same time by saying, "Nutin' much. Just enjoyin' another day." One of the guys said, "I hear you're looking for the Blues." I responded, "I'm on my way to do a show up here."

Before I could say more, another one of the guys said, "I know you. You're on your way to do a tribute to Elvis." I asked him how he knew that, and he said, "There's some things you just know."

I learned that one of the guys playing guitar was a brother of Muddy Waters. We sang the old song, "Baby, What You Want?" by Jimmy Reed. I told them that Elvis had actually sung that song in his 1968 come-back special, and several of them remembered that. We sang "Don't Be Cruel" and "Hound Dog" in a shuffle, Blues way. One of them remarked that Chuck Berry had said Elvis was the best that ever was or will be. (Chuck Berry was the pioneer of rock 'n roll, and the first man to ever record a rock 'n roll song.)

Then I sat and listened while they told me stories of the difficulties of growing up poor in this area of the country and of learning to live with little. Famous people came out of Mississippi because they dreamed big. They thought Elvis was black the first time they heard him, and felt he was an ambassador to get their Blues music out to the market. They all liked Elvis because he went out of his way to help others. I didn't get names of the other guys, but they were all famous Blues musicians.

After leaving the guys I went to the local convenience store and told them about my meeting with the four guys. They said they were certain most of those guys were dead. I said, "That can't be true. I was just down the street a little way and played and sang with those guys." Finally one of the locals who had lived in Rolling Forks all his life said that if those men were really in town, they hadn't been seen together in about fifteen years, and I must have been fortunate enough to experience a rare occasion of them all being together.

That chance meeting reminded me of the Robert Johnson song, "Cross Roads Blues." I never actually saw the man who said to me, "We are the Blues," yet he pointed me to the group of old Blues musicians with whom I shared an incredible hour of music and insight into Blues history.

Welcome To Louisiana. One of the most haunted and mysterious states in the United States, it has a rich heritage of French and Native American culture along with the slave roots of the French Creoles from the Caribbean and the Acadian culture from Nova Scotia French Canadians

Elvis' debut at the Louisiana Hayride on October 16, 1954

(Cajuns). Louisiana claims to be the birthplace of Jazz and the stomping grounds for Blues music.

What does Louisiana have to do with Elvis Presley and Shea Arender? Well, Elvis' career was launched in Shreveport, Louisiana in 1954. At age nineteen, one month after his initial performance at the Shreveport Louisiana Hayride, he signed a year long contract to perform every Saturday night there.

Elvis' favorite movie of himself, "King Creole," was filmed in 1958 in New Orleans, Louisiana. This was Elvis' last attempt to make his mark on the 1950s before serving a term in the U.S. Army. The music in the movie had Louisiana flavor, but retained the Jazz, Dixieland and Rockabilly, up-tempo boogie style to which Elvis was accustomed. No other artist had successfully blended these arrangements together. Many critics consider this to be his best film as well as his most successful film statistically.

I was born in Vicksburg, Mississippi, but moved to Louisiana at age four and lived there until my graduation from High School. My aunt's family had a place in the French Quarter, a short distance from where the movie "King Creole" was filmed. My aunt loved Louisiana, Elvis, and "King Creole." It was a blast to visit downtown New Orleans and spend time with family and friends. I grew up hearing stories of how "King Creole" was filmed and the excitement of my aunt's friends over meeting Elvis.

I come from a background of Baptist and Catholic Church roots. New Orleans is deeply rooted in Roman Catholicism, which is not nearly as widespread in north Mississippi and Memphis where Elvis was native. As a young boy, I remember people from local restaurants telling me stories of how Elvis would come in there and ask many questions about religion, and Catholicism in particular. Elvis grew up in the Assembly of God Church. According to my aunt's friend, Ema Landry, he wasn't just trying to make conversation. He listened attentively as though he was attending a religious lecture, and he absorbed every word of it. It is possible that Elvis' small stint in New Orleans opened his eyes to other religions, and after the death of his mother, he became obsessed with reading everything he could find on that subject.

Several years ago while passing through New Orleans, I visited the vicinity of the French Quarter where "King Creole" was filmed. I stood on the sidewalk and reminisced about stories my aunt had told me of Elvis going to the nearby restaurant after filming, to relax and interact with the locals. Suddenly, my thoughts were interrupted by some of the locals who proceeded to relate some interesting legends about the area.

They told me that I didn't want to be walking around that area at night because it was haunted. There had been reports of ghost sightings and voices coming from an abandoned building. People wondered if some-one had been abused in times past in that building because the voices seemed to say the words, "Hard-headed woman."

Instantly my curiosity was piqued. I asked them if they were aware that Elvis had starred in a movie in the 1950s in that very area, and one of the songs he had sung in the movie was called "Hard-Headed Woman." They were not aware of those facts. Although I've always thought of New Orleans as being a city of mystery and intrigue, the chance encounter that day gave me a little glimpse into the folklore and spiritual forces at work in the area.

Chapter 7

The Experience – Performing Elvis Tributes

Getting Started

Elvis Presley has been a household name for as long as I can remember. My mother gave me Elvis' Golden Records when I was seven years old. I would listen to them for hours, memorizing the lyrics and the enunciation of each word in the songs. I did my first Elvis performance in school at age seven. I remember another time at age seven when I sang Elvis' song, "Hound Dog" on the school bus after returning to school from a class field trip.

My first serious Elvis performance before a large crowd of people took place aboard a Commodore Cruise Ship in the Caribbean at age twelve. From that point forward, I knew that I wanted to be a performer of Elvis music. I studied everything I could find about Elvis, and listened to his music and watched his movies.

The next six years found me performing in local shows and festivals, in addition to occasional guest concert performances across the South. During the summer of 1996, at age sixteen, I was invited to perform an Elvis show on a cruise ship. I continued doing the Elvis cruise ship performances during the summers of the next two years. During my three summers on the cruise ships, I met many people from other countries and developed an interest in studying languages.

In January of 2002 I entered and won a World Elvis Tribute competition. There were more international entrants than there were Americans. The finalist competition took place on a cruise ship in Miami. The prize was $5000 cash, the title of World Champion Elvis Tribute, and a trophy.

Italy

My college studies in Italian music and opera took me to Venice, Italy in the summer of 2002. Because of the recognition I had received earlier in the year in the World Elvis Tribute competition, my music agency was able to arrange for me to perform some Elvis shows during the three months I was in Italy.

I went to classes during the day and did some concerts and guest appearances on other people's shows during the weekday evenings. But my favorite performances in Italy took place on the weekends in several Italian clubs in the vicinity of a little community called the Grado. The Fonzari Hotel featured our Elvis Tribute show every weekend over the course of a month. The shows were presented in a variety show format, featuring performers from various musical genres. Some of the featured music was Italian pop/rock, American jam band and just to top it off, a tribute to Elvis. A majority of the entertainers performed without a set list of songs for their segment of the evening, which produced a very informal atmosphere. We might perform a song for fourteen minutes because we were trying to see how many guitar solos we could fit into one song.

The promoters of my Elvis shows in Italy created posters featuring an illusional photo of Elvis in the background along with a photo of myself in front. This creation became the standard format for my advertising in future years. It was a way of showcasing me as a Solo/Tribute Artist rather than an unidentifiable American impersonator in a jumpsuit. The Italian advertising was great for me since I was in the early stages of becoming a Tribute Artist rather than an unidentifiable impersonator.

The crowds in Italy are crazy. The louder we played, the wilder the crowds became. Europeans are more open sexually than Americans, and many star-struck girls would pull their tops off in response to the loud, energetic music. Once one girl started it, the fad spread like wildfire throughout the crowd. The security personnel would let the charade go on until the girls would try to charge the stage, at which point they were intercepted and escorted out.

Shows began at 10:00 pm and lasted until around 5:00 am. The hotel pro-prietors approved of our loud, lengthy performances because the longer we performed, the more drinks they sold to the audience. After all the performers had finished their scheduled performances, then we would get together, chug champagne, and sing whatever we wanted to sing to each other. We sang Frank Sinatra, Tony Bennett and some American soul classics as well. Often, our after-the-show merry-making prohib-ited us from being able to distinguish between Bennett and Sinatra. It was expected that we would try different wines, for turning them down when offered was considered a little rude in Italy. Not wanting to offend my hosts, I continued to have a few more. On one of those occasions, I became bold enough to try to sing Pavarotti.

When we finally left the hotel around 5:00 am, we were still so pumped up from the adrenaline rush of the evening that it was impossible to go to bed. Sometimes we went to the nearby beach to hang out. Other times we would sing and dance in the old brick streets of the quaint little town while carrying our wine bottles and acoustic guitars. I would start singing in Italian, and the local musicians there would tell me to stick with Elvis! Everyone would be laughing, and our conversations would become a mixture of English and Italian. Finally, the frivolity would cease as exhaustion overcame us, and we'd return to our rooms for some sleep.

Once we came down from the emotional "high," we were overwhelmed with feelings of aloneness. Entertaining can have the same effect as a drug. When you're hearing the adulation of the crowds as they scream your name, that adrenaline rush produces abnormal bursts of energy, causing a more frenzied performance to prolong the "high." However, once the screaming fans have gone home, and your body settles back into its regular hormonal rhythms, the loneliness is acute. Having a few friends around you during these times does not prevent the plunge from ecstasy to despair. Unless a person has been an entertainer/musician, they may not be able to understand the severe mental drain that occurs after a performance. During those periods of emptiness, I would always think about an Elvis article from a 1977 Memphis newspaper in which the statement was made that, "a lonely life ends on Elvis Presley Boulevard." I discussed that article with the guys in the band, and we all agreed with the truth of the statement. It took me almost fifteen years in the business to fully understand that cycle of ecstasy and loneliness, but now that I do, I've learned ways to cope with it. We always liked to think that Elvis, in spite of his unparalleled success, made huge sacrifices to pave the way for all of us in the entertainment world who would come after him.

Brazil

While in Italy I received a call from one of my agents saying I had been invited to take my Elvis show to Brazil during the Christmas holidays. I continued with my college studies upon returning home from Italy, and during my Christmas break, I traveled to a small town in northeast Brazil for two weeks of concerts.

The weather at Christmas in Brazil was comparable to our summer season in the northern hemisphere, although it wasn't hot like Mississippi and Louisiana summers. Because American entertainers were somewhat of a rarity in this small Brazilian town, there was a lot of television and media involvement. Due to the heavy advertising, the event was well attended.

All of the concerts were held outdoors. The people in Brazil have a great appreciation for Elvis' music. I would see the listeners mouthing the words as I sang, although I doubt they understood the meaning of the songs. Every so often I would confuse them by inserting some Portuguese words into my singing.

These events were very high-energy, and the crowds were on their feet, clapping, cheering, and screaming my name during the entire performance. The ages of the crowds were pretty mixed between old and young. The younger set responded to the loud, fast-paced music, but at the end of the loud, foot-stomping songs, the older folks would request that I sing some Elvis Gospel songs.

Las Vegas

Although I've taken my Elvis Tribute Shows around the world, my absolute favorite place to perform in the United States is Las Vegas. Elvis performed at the Las Vegas Hotel Hilton between the years of 1969-1977, so there is a huge appreciation for his music in this city. He would do two shows each evening: one at 8:15 pm and the second one at midnight.

The shows in Las Vegas are more formal than the ones I did in Italy and Brazil. The audience will occasionally receive a program with a list of songs to be performed, and each show lasts approximately one hour.

Although I've performed at various places in Las Vegas, one of my favorite venues to stop in is the Casa di Amore Italian Restaurant. This is not just an ordinary eating place. It's kind of like a dinner theater, with live entertainment while the customers eat and drink. This place has the distinction of being the scene of the laughter and loving memories of the beloved Rat Pack. Yes, this is the place where Frank Sinatra, Peter Lawford, Joey Bishop, Humphrey Bogart, Dean Martin, Sammy Davis, Jr., and even Tony Bennett and Elvis would spend many after-concert hours singing encores, talking and rejoicing about life. The staff there always treats us so well, and we enjoy performing there. The crowds are more traditional Las Vegas rather than the new crowd in other places. However, it's still a good mixture.

In 2009, my parents joined me in Las Vegas, and we celebrated my dad's eightieth birthday at the Casa di Amore. I did a guest appearance that evening with a crooner by the name of George Bugati. The crowd that night was very emotional, and we performed a number of love ballads, which my parents loved. Typically, I would close my shows with "American Trilogy."

The Elvis song that impacts me the most is "My Way." Even the crowd gets very emotional when I sing this song. In this song, I really sense Elvis' presence. People have even stated that my voice changes as I lock into the Elvis feeling. Singing "My Way" tends to produce an "out-of-body" experience. It seems I can almost see Elvis with tears in his eyes, reaching out for something to soothe the pain and sadness due to the losses in his life.

Chapter 8

Shea as Elvis

Hardships and Rewards

All my life I've experienced serious pressure in my role as an Elvis Tribute Artist. At times it can be overwhelming. Every crowd ranges from extreme critics to fanatical fans of Elvis. My vocal performance and looks are constantly being assessed and compared to Elvis. There are those who love everything I do. Then there is the opposite extreme of those who hate everything. I've learned many lessons through the years in dealing with people. Obviously, I can't please everyone every time, so I've learned that I must be happy with myself and the job I'm doing.

Through my journeys, I have found there are Elvis fans worldwide. I sing Elvis songs in English as he sang them, and even if the audience can't speak English very well, they still seem to shout out the song lyrics. Elvis has international appeal, because unlike America, other countries still put Elvis memorabilia in the mainstream media. For example, even though he's dead, he still continues to chart hits internationally.

Elvis was and continues to be the biggest selling artist of all time. He is the only artist in the history of music to chart hits in every country worldwide. His sound was so diverse, as he recorded in Country, Rock, Jazz, Blues, Dixieland and Gospel. With Elvis, there was something for everybody. He was loved by people of all races -- and all ages. Even children were fascinated by his costumes and his stage presence.

The rewards of paying tribute to one of the greatest entertainers of all time have greatly outweighed any hardships I've experienced. We have traveled around the world and met some wonderful people on our journey. For this I feel thankful and very blessed.

Typical Set List for Formal Shows

<u>Shea Arender's Tribute to Elvis Set List</u>

Opening Vamp
CC Rider
Love Me
You Gave me a Mountain
Blue Moon
Blue Suede Shoes
For the Good Times
Teddy Bear / Don't be Cruel
Prelude Piano Intro/ My Way
It's Now or Never
Never Been To Spain
Kentucky Rain
Treat Me Nice

Trouble
Baby What You Want Me To Do
Jailhouse Medley
Fever
In the Ghetto
A Little Less Conversation
Burning Love
Suspicious Minds
American Trilogy
Can't Help Falling in Love (Fast Concert Version)
Closing Vamp

Typical Set List for Rockabilly Shows

Shea Arender's Tribute to Elvis Set List

That's All Right Mama
Blue Swede Shoes
Blue Moon
Mystery Train
Loving You
Baby Let's Play House
Don't Be Cruel / Hound Dog

Teddy Bear
Peace In The Valley
Trouble
Love Me Tender
All Shook Up
Blue Christmas (seasonal)
Jailhouse Rock Medley

After live concerts Shea meets and greets his fans.

Shea Arender - Live in Concert

One man legends show, Ricky Nelson, Dean Martin and Elvis

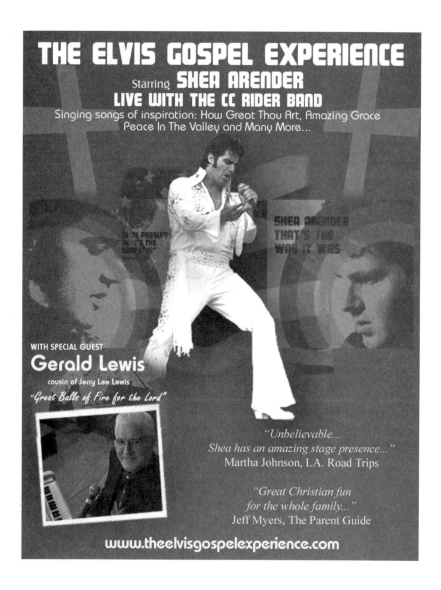

Shea Arender - Live in Concert

Shea Arender - Live in Concert

Chapter 9

Where Were You? Elvis' Concert History

Elvis' Tour Schedule from his famous "1968 Comeback Special" to his "1973 Aloha From Hawaii"

1968 "1968 Comeback Special" - The Famous Black Leather Suit. This awesome TV concert seen by more than 75 million people worldwide, aired in December, 1968. It was the first live performance for Presley in more than 7 years.

1969 July 31 - August 28th - International Hotel in Las Vegas. Two shows a day. Most at 8:15 pm and at midnight. All sold out to capacity.

1970 January 26th - February 23rd - International Hotel in Las Vegas. Two shows a day. Most at 8:15 pm and at midnight. All sold out to capacity.

Date	Location	City / State	Time	Crowd[1]	Suit
Feb. 27, 1970	Houston Astrodome	Houston TX	2:00 pm	16708	White Cossack Top Suit
Feb. 27, 1970	Houston Astrodome	Houston TX	7:45 pm	36299	Thin Green Leaf suit
Feb. 28, 1970	Houston Astrodome	Houston TX	2:00 pm	37733	Blue Brocade Suit
Feb. 28, 1970	Houston Astrodome	Houston TX	7:45 pm	43614	White Brocade Suit
Mar. 1, 1970	Houston Astrodome	Houston TX	2:00 pm	40858	White Cossack Top Suit
Mar. 1, 1970	Houston Astrodome	Houston TX	7:00 pm	27777	White Brocade Suit

1970   August 10th – September 8th - International Hotel in Las Vegas. Two shows a day. Most at 8:15 pm and at midnight. All sold to capacity.

Date	Venue	City/ State	Showtime	Crowd	Suit worn
Sept. 9, 1970	Veteran Memorial Coliseum	Phoenix AZ	8:30 pm	13300	Fringe suit
Sept. 10, 1970	Kiel Auditorium	St Louis MO	8:30 pm	12000	Chain Suit
Sept. 11, 1970	Olympia Stadium	Detroit MI	8:30 pm	16000	Chain Suit
Sept. 12, 1970	Convention Center	Miami FL	3:00 pm	12000	Fringe suit
Sept. 12, 1970	Convention Center	Miami FL	8:30 pm	12000	Chain Suit

1   All crowd numbers are estimates. All Elvis Presley Vegas shows and indoor arena shows were sold out to capacity. Some numbers may reflect overflow numbers if there were two shows in the same night.

110

Sept. 13, 1970	Curtis Hixon Hall	Tampa FL	3:00 pm	7500	Chain Suit
Sept. 13, 1970	Curtis Hixon Hall	Tampa FL	8:30 pm	7500	Metal Eye Suit
Sept. 14, 1970	Municipal Auditorium	Mobile AL	8:30 pm	10800	Fringe suit

Date	Venue	City/ State	Showtime	Crowd	Suit
Nov. 10, 1970	Oakland Coliseum	Oakland CA	8:30 pm	14000	White Nail suit
Nov. 11, 1970	Memorial Coliseum	Portland OR	8:30 pm	11800	Lace suit
Nov. 12, 1970	Coliseum	Seattle WA	8:30 pm	15000	Fringe suit
Nov. 13, 1970	Cow Palace	San Francisco CA	8:30 pm	14300	Red Ladder suit
Nov. 14, 1970	The Forum	Los Angeles CA	3:00 pm	18700	White Nail suit
Nov. 14, 1970	The Forum	Los Angeles CA	8:30 pm	18698	Wing suit
Nov. 15, 1970	Sports Arena	San Diego CA	8:30 pm	14659	Chain Suit
Nov. 16, 1970	Fair Ground Arena	Oklahoma City OK	8:30 pm	11000	Lace suit
Nov. 17, 1970	Denver Coliseum	Denver CO	8:30 pm	12000	Fringe suit

1971   January 26th – February 23rd - International Hotel in Las Vegas. Two shows a day. Most at 8:15 pm and at midnight. All sold to capacity.

111

1971 July 20th – August 2nd - Sahara Hotel in Lake Tahoe, NV. Two shows a day. Most at 10:00 pm and at midnight.

1971 August 9th - September 6th - International Hotel in Las Vegas. Two shows a day. Most shows at 8:15 pm and at midnight.

Date	Venue	City/State	Showtime	Crowd	Suit worn
Nov. 5, 1971	Metropolitan Sports Center	Minneapolis MN	8:30 pm	17600	White Matador suit
Nov. 6, 1971	Public Hall Auditorium	Cleveland OH	2:30 pm	10000	Black Matador suit
Nov. 6, 1971	Public Hall Auditorium	Cleveland OH	8:30 pm	10000	White Matador suit
Nov. 7, 1971	Fair & Expo C	Louisville KY	2:30 pm	18550	White Fireworks suit
Nov. 8, 1971	Spectrum	Philadelphia PA	8:30 pm	16601	White Spectrum suit
Nov. 9, 1971	Civic Center	Baltimore MD	8:30 pm	12228	White Matador suit
Nov. 10, 1971	Boston Garden	Boston MA	8:30 pm	15509	Black Matador suit
Nov. 11, 1971	Cincinnati Garden	Cincinnati OH	8:30 pm	13272	Black Fireworks suit
Nov. 12, 1971	Hofheinz Pavillon	Houston TX	8:30 pm	12000	White Matador suit
Nov. 13, 1971	Memorial Auditorium	Dallas TX	2:30 pm	10000	Black Fireworks suit
Nov. 13, 1971	Memorial Auditorium	Dallas TX	8:30 pm	10000	White Spectrum suit
Nov. 14, 1971	University of Alabama	Tuscaloosa AL	2:30 pm	12000	Black Matador suit
Nov. 15, 1971	Municipal Auditorium	Kansas City MO	8:30 pm	10400	White Matador suit
Nov. 16, 1971	Salt Palace	Salt Lake City UT	8:30 pm	13000	White Spectrum suit

1972 January 26th - February 23rd - Hilton Hotel in Las Vegas. Two shows a day. Most shows at 8:15 pm and at midnight.

Date	Venue	City/State	Showtime	Crowd	Suit worn
April 5, 1972	Memorial Auditorium	Buffalo NY	8:30 pm	17360	Blue Nail suit
April 6, 1972	Olympia Stadium	Detroit MI	8:30 pm	16216	White Matador suit
April 7, 1972	University of Dayton	Dayton OH	8:30 pm	13788	White Fireworks suit
April 8, 1972	UOT Arena	Knoxville TN	2:30 pm	10500	White Spectrum suit
April 8, 1972	UOT Arena	Knoxville TN	8:30 pm	13300	Blue Nail suit
April 9, 1972	Hampton Roads Coliseum	Hampton VA	2:30 pm	11000	Red Matador suit
April 9, 1972	Hampton Roads Coliseum	Hampton VA	8:30 pm	10650	Blue Nail suit
April 10, 1972	Richmond Coliseum	Richmond VA	8:30 pm	11500	Red Matador suit
April 11, 1972	Civic Center Coliseum	Roanoke VA	8:30 pm	10436	White Matador suit
April 12, 1972	Fair Grounds Col	Indianapolis IN	8:30 pm	11000	Blue Nail Suit
April 13, 1972	Charlotte Coliseum	Charlotte NC	8:30 pm	12000	White Fireworks suit
April 14, 1972	Greensboro Coliseum	Greensboro NC	8:30 pm	16300	Royal Blue Fireworks suit
April 15, 1972	Macon Coliseum	Macon GA	2:30 pm	11500	White Spectrum suit

April 15, 1972	Macon Coliseum	Macon GA	8:30 pm	11500	White Matador suit
April 16, 1972	Veterans Memorial Coliseum	Jacksonville FL	2:30 pm	9258	White Pyramid suit
April 16, 1972	Veterans Memorial Coliseum	Jacksonville FL	(8:30 pm)	9500	Blue Nail suit
April 17, 1972	T.H. Barton Coliseum	Little Rock AR	(8:30 pm)	10000	Red Matador suit
April 18, 1972	Convention Center	San Antonio TX	(8:30 pm)	10500	White Matador suit
April 19, 1972	Tingley Coliseum	Albuquerque NM	(8:30 pm)	11847	White Fireworks suit

Date	Venue	City/State	Showtime	Crowd	Suit worn
June 9, 1972	Madison Square Garden	New York NY	8:30 pm	20000	Adonis suit
June 10, 1972	Madison Square Garden	New York NY	2:30 pm	20000	Blue Cluster suit
June 10, 1972	Madison Square Garden	New York NY	8:30 pm	20000	Double Porthole suit
June 11, 1972	Madison Square Garden	New York NY	2:30 pm	20000	Double Porthole suit
June 12, 1972	Memorial Coliseum	Fort Wayne IN	8:30 pm	7690	Blue Swirl suit
June 13, 1972	Roberts Memorial Stadium	Evansville IN	8:30 pm	11500	Blue Cluster suit

June 14, 1972	Auditorium Arena	Milwaukee WI	8:30 pm	10559	Adonis suit
June 15, 1972	Auditorium Arena	Milwaukee WI	8:30 pm	11600	Blue Nail suit
June 16, 1972	Chicago Stadium	Chicago IL	8:30 pm	20000	Adonis suit
June 17, 1972	Chicago Stadium	Chicago IL	2:30 pm	15000	White Two-Piece suit with Black Pockets
June 17, 1972	Chicago Stadium	Chicago IL	8:30 pm	20000	Blue Nail suit
June 18, 1972	Tarrant Count Center	Fort Worth TX	8:30 pm	14122	Double Porthole suit
June 19, 1972	Henry Levitt Arena	Wichita KS	8:30 pm	10000	White Two-Piece suit with Black Pockets
June 20, 1972	Civic Assembly Center	Tulsa OK	8:30 pm	9500	White Two-Piece suit with Laced Pockets

1972 August 4th – September 4th - Hilton Hotel in Las Vegas. Two shows a day. Most shows at 8:15 pm and midnight. All sold to capacity.

Date	Venue	City/State	Showtime	Crowd	Suit Worn
Nov. 8, 1972	Municipal Coliseum	Lubbock TX	8:30 pm	10000	Blue Nail suit
Nov. 9, 1972	Community C Arena	Tucson AZ	8:30 pm	9700	Adonis suit
Nov. 10, 1972	Coliseum	El Paso TX	8:30 pm	9000	Red Matador suit
Nov. 11, 1972	Oakland Coliseum	Oakland CA	8:30 pm	14000	Thunderbird suit

Nov. 12, 1972	Swing Auditorium	San Bernardino CA	5:00 pm	7200	Black Conquistador suit
Nov. 13, 1972	Swing Auditorium	San Bernardino CA	8:30 pm	7200	Royal Blue Fireworks suit
Nov. 14, 1972	Long Beach Arena	Long Beach CA	8:30 pm	14000	Tiffany suit
Nov. 15, 1972	Long Beach Arena	Long Beach CA	8:30 pm	14000	Saturn suit
Nov. 17, 1972	The H.I.C. Arena	Honolulu HI	8:30 pm	8400	Thunderbird suit
Nov. 18, 1972	The H.I.C. Arena	Honolulu HI	2:30 pm	8400	Black Conquistador suit
Nov. 18, 1972	The H.I.C. Arena	Honolulu HI	8:30 pm	9000	Tiffany suit

1973 "Aloha from Hawaii" - The biggest Live TV concert in History to this day. It was seen by 1.5 billion people worldwide.

Photo courtesy of www.freeclassicimages.com

Photo courtesy of www.freeclassicimages.com

Photo courtesy of www.freeclassicimages.com

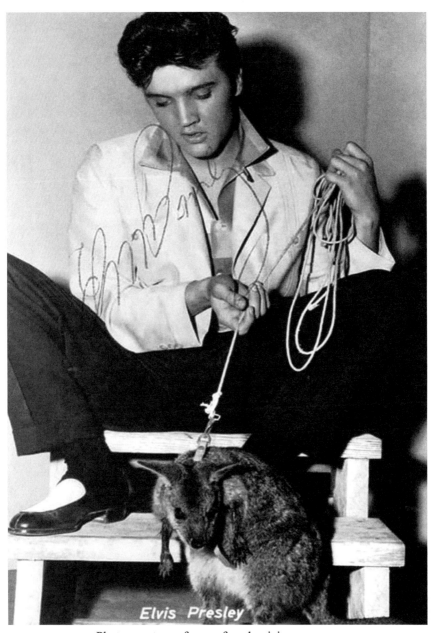

Photo courtesy of www.freeclassicimages.com

Photo courtesy of www.freeclassicimages.com

Author Bio

Arender has a degree in international business and is also educated in music theory, vocalization, song writing and Classical forms. Arender has taken his love for music all over the world.

One of the most diverse and select artists in the world that effortlessly combines musical genres – from Jazz Standards, Classic Rock, R&B, Blues, Love Ballads, to Country Music – into the same concert – SHEA ARENDER brings an electrifying, super-charged journey of harmony and musical illusions to the stage.

Musical genres and geographic borders do not limit this high-octane baritone vocalist and singer/songwriter. Shea Arender, who studied opera in Grado, Italy, and who sings in Spanish and Portuguese, has performed throughout the United States as well as in Brazil, Italy and Puerto Rico.

An imaginative Entertainer and singer capable of putting his own sway on many artists' songs, but has perfected Elvis Presley's classic material, Arender's performances as a tribute to Elvis have brought him accolades and worldwide attention. A former world champion for his tribute to

Presley's performances, Arender starred as Elvis in the nationwide tour, formerly known as ABC's Next Best Thing. He is no stranger to major cinematic productions; Shea has also appeared in "Mission Impossible" movie events as Tom Cruise.

In elegance and mystery, Arender connects with the fans who have made it all possible every time he takes the stage, delivering performances in a sometimes romantic, comedic and always confident style that is uniquely his own.

Shea Arender, who first headlined a show when he was twelve years old, constantly finds new ways to express himself artistically with songwriting and legendary illusions. His performance evokes passion for life and heart-felt poignancy. Arender arranges, produces and choreographs his remarkable cinematic concerts. His fearless performances are guaranteed to make "Believers" out of his audiences.

Shea Arender

For bookings and more artist information contact:

Global Entertainment Inc.
www.GlobalEntertainmentInc.net

Shea Arender

Shea Arender American Trilogy
Order your copy at:

www.SheaAsElvis.com
www.SheaArender.com

Visit Shea on Facebook and Twitter